Basic Gardening

Basic Gardening

Stanley B. Whitehead

Ward Lock Limited · London

First published in Great Britain in 1977
by Ward Lock Limited, 116 Baker Street,
London W1M 2BB, a member of the Pentos
Group.

House editor Teresa Mozley

Layout by Jacqueline Ashdown

Printed and bound in Great Britain by
Cox & Wyman Ltd
London Fakenham Reading

British Library Cataloguing in Publication Data

Whitehead, Stanley Bamford
   Basic gardening — (Concorde books)
   1. Gardening
   I. Title   II. Series
   635   SB453

   ISBN 0–7063–5369–2
   ISBN 0–7063–5371–4   Pbk

Contents

1 Keys to Gardening Success 7

2 Know Your Soil 13

3 Planning and Planting 32

4 Planning the Open Spaces 43

5 Tooling Up 49

6 Hedging for Shelter and Ornament 55

7 Planting for Permanence 60

8 For Instant Flowering 72

9 Value from Vegetables 77

10 Tree Fruits, Soft Fruits and Strawberries 83

11 Keeping the Garden Healthy 94

Index 103

1
Keys to Gardening Success

Gardening is simply the cultivation of plants. It becomes complicated when the plants we want to grow, whether for pleasure or reward, come from elsewhere—other climes or other countries—or are selected forms, varieties or hybrids non-existent previously in the wild.

THE NATURE OF PLANTS

Plants, like ourselves, are living organisms, complex assemblies of cells, ranging from the uni-cellular links of the algae that green a pond to the multi-cellular structures of trees that become dominant where nature has full say.

Plants feed on inorganic mineral matter and transform it into organised cellular material that can nourish animal life in its many forms, directly in the case of the herbivores, indirectly in the case of the carnivores. At the same time, plants have made this planet a more or less congenial place where animal life can develop and thrive. Without plants, life as we know it would not be, and the earth a barren waste.

Botanists usually group the plant or vegetable kingdom into thirteen divisions. Twelve of these contain the non-flowering plants or Cryptogams (algae, bacteria, fungi, diatoms, lichens, liverworts, mosses, ferns, etc) with which we are likely to have only passing acquaintance. Excepting ferns and their allies, they are seldom cultivated as garden plants.

The thirteenth division consists of the flowering plants or Phanerogams and includes the vast number of green foliaged and stemmed garden plants. This division is split further into two sub-divisions—the woody plants which have their seed structures or ovules exposed, called the Gymnospermae, and include the conifers (firs, cypresses, pines and yews); and the plants which have their ovules in a closed container or ovary, and are known as the Angiospermae; including all the colourful garden flowers and food crop plants; and a majority of the plants we call weeds.

In turn, the angiosperms may be divided into two classes—those which on germination push up only one seed-leaf or cotyledon and are thus known as monocotyledons; and those emerging with two seed leaves, the dicotyledons. The plants have also significant differences in development which should be of interest to the observant gardener. Monocotyledons form a tufted, fibrous root system, their leaves have veins of equal thickness running parallel, and their flowers have their parts in threes, or multiples of three. The dicotyledons form a main central tap-root, from which side roots of lesser thickness develop; their leaves have a main vein, with many side branching veins forming a net-work.

Because of the nature of their root systems, dicotyledonous plants tend to be more deeply rooting than the monocotyledonous, and need deep soils to grow well.

THE GROWTH NEEDS OF PLANTS

All green plants have five vital needs which must be met if they are to live, grow healthily and successfully complete their life cycle. They need:

Air   like all living organisms plants must breathe.

Light   indispensable for the energy it provides to spark the manufacture of foodstuffs, particularly carbohydrates (sugars and starches) by the photosynthesis of carbon, hydrogen and oxygen present in the air and water taken in by the plant.

Water   needed as the solvent to carry nutrient mineral elements to the leaves and to distribute foodstuffs within the plant, to maintain cell turgidity and growth processes, and to provide some of the elements, chiefly hydrogen and oxygen.

Warmth   temperatures govern the rate at which bio-chemical reactions take place within the plant, and therefore the rate of growth. Falling temperatures slow growth, rising quicken, but very few garden plants can survive 0°C/32°F for very long.

Nutrient elements   these are needed to make the substance of the plant and to keep it healthy. Most of the substance of a plant comes from the air and water it absorbs. They fill its cells and tissues and provide the raw materials of the sugars and starches that confribute to its bulk. But for the actual manu-facture of plant structure and maintenance of function a number of nutrient elements are needed, and these come very largely from the rooting medium or soil.

At least twelve elements are essential for healthy plant growth. Some are needed in relatively large quantities and are termed the macro-nutrients or major elements and include nitrogen, phosphorus, potassium, calcium, sulphur and iron; others, needed in relatively small or trace amounts are the micro-nutrients or trace elements and include manganese, boron, copper, zinc and molybdenum. There are other elements which are beneficial to certain plants, such as aluminium, chlorine, silicon and sodium, but not vital to growth; and plants can absorb elements which may be toxic or of no useful purpose to them.

Some plants, such as alpines, need clearer, purer air than others to grow well. Plants vary in their light tolerances, some growing best in open sun, others in various degrees of shade. Some plants, notably cacti and succulents, thrive in the dry soils of deserts; others such as water-lilies are wholly aquatic. Most plants have a conditioned tolerance to warmth. Plants of tropical origin do not survive in cool temperate conditions, and even sub-tropical plants, sometimes termed half-hardy, do not survive low temperatures unless from high altitudes.

The performance of plants is also greatly affected by their in-built tolerance to soil conditions and their mineral resources. An outstanding example is the rhododendron and many of its relatives of the *Ericaceae* or Heath family which can only thrive in soils free of lime.

One of the major differences between animals and plants is that plants have no real mobility. They have to grow where we put them. They may show escapist inclinations in light-seeking elongation of their shoots or roots lengthening woodily through poor soil, but basically they have to put up with what their immediate environment provides.

It would be too much to say that plants adapt to conditions. They don't. They do have certain tolerances, but the nearer they have to grow to the limits in air, light, water, temperature and nutritional needs, the poorer their performance and chances of survival. Most garden plants are exotic either by origin or breeding. The humble potato had its origins in South America. Even native plants are garden-grown in selected and developed forms, and a surprising number of our best ornamental and flowering plants have arisen within the captivity of cultivated gardens.

ASSESSING GARDEN CHARACTERISTICS

The start of good gardening lies in correctly assessing the characteristics and qualities of the area to be cultivated in relation to plant needs. You can do it mentally if your memory holds facts well, but better still make a plan, outlining your boundaries and their natures, your buildings, and any permanent difficult-to-alter things like manholes. If you use squared paper, you can work to an agreed scale, and with an accompanying notebook, have an invaluable record and guide for future years. The factors which will influence your gardening progress are:

Climate Apart from the overall influence of the climate of the country or region in which you garden, the play of the elements—sun, wind, rain, light, etc—as they bear on your own particular domain, is influential and to be noted. Latitude affects temperatures, and the daily intensity and duration of light. The farther north you are, in the northern hemisphere at least, the lower these are, especially at the beginning and end of the annual growing season. Spring comes two to three weeks earlier in southern regions than in northern; while autumn comes to the north earlier than to the south.

This not only means you can sow and plant earlier in the south and enjoy prolonged cropping and flowering, but that you can grow a wider range of plants. In the north early-flowering and tender growth may be marred by the last flurries of winter, and late flowering or late maturing plants caught out by autumnal chill. Plants hardy enough in southern parts may not have the same hardiness in the north with a shorter growing season and less sun and warmth; a point to bear in mind especially when selecting shrubs and trees.

Longitude often has a bearing on climate. Over Great Britain, the prevailing winds come from the south-west, carrying with them rains off the Atlantic Oceans. The western half of our islands, therefore, enjoy a more moist and some-what gentler climate than the eastern, and on this account is often a better home for many plants. Particularly, as the dryness of the east is often compounded by chilling north and east winds from the continent.

Location   Exactly where a garden is located in relation to the physical character of surrounding topography is of some significance. Nearness to the sea or a large lake modifies humidity and temperatures. This is particularly true of the western coasts from Cornwall to Ross and Cromarty touched by the Gulf Stream, where many gardens, famous for their variety of plants, are found. Coastal gardens are also subject to salt-laden winds, needing a first line of defence of plants chosen for their salt resistance.

Altitude and the position of a garden in the land need to be noted. The higher above sea level, the lower the range of temperatures, and barometric pressures, and the greater the exposure to wind and inclement weather—dictating a need for plants of a hardy nature. A garden in a valley or low-lying stretch or pocket of land may be less exposed to rough, forceful weather, but vulnerable to frosts, since cold air flows to and accumulates at such low points. On sloping ground, cold air currents tend to move down and through a garden with more transient effect, but aspect, whether to a damper west, a colder north, a drier east or a warmer south, also affects garden climate, and must be taken into account.

Soil   Plants begin life in soil, and at least half, often more, of their lives and functions in it, as root systems. A soil must provide good anchorage and stability to a plant if its roots are to grow and function effectively. These largely depend upon a soil's texture, porosity and depth which determine how readily roots can penetrate and extend. Secondly, a plant needs a more or less constant supply of water together with a range of essential water-soluble mineral nutrients being regularly available in good balance. Other things being equal, a plant is as good as its soil; for it basically determines how well a plant is nourished and maintained.

2
Know Your Soil

Soil is the thin surface skin of earth that forms on the rock mantle of this planet when subject to increasing fragmentation by climatic erosion, wetted and mixed with the decomposing remains of the various forms of organisms, plant and animal, that evolve on and in it. As such, it consists of (1) the inorganic mineral particles coming from the parent rocks; (2) particles of organic matter from dead plants and animals; (3) water from rains or snow; (4) air from the atmosphere; and (5) living organisms, such as algae, fungi, bacteria, earthworms, molluscs and various insects with their predators.

Closely mixed together, the soil's components give rise to a complex bio-chemical ferment from which the most important result is the release of soluble mineral nutrient elements to the soil moisture to form a nutrient solution on which plant roots can draw. A prime objective in gardening is to cultivate the soil so as to maximise this result.

THE MINERAL MAKE-UP

The mineral particles which make up a soil are its most permanent part and give it physical texture, and basic characteristics. They vary considerably in size, from stones to ultra-microscopic specks. Most soils contain a mixture in which the different sizes of particles vary greatly in their proportions, and so do much to determine the type of soil and its nature. They are the source of several mineral salts or plant nutrients, but the smaller the particles, the more chemically reactive they are.

These particles can be conveniently divided into five categories—gravel and stones, with particles larger than 2mm (millimetres); coarse sand, with particles smaller than 2mm, and larger than 0.2mm; fine sand, with particles smaller than 0.2mm and larger than 0.02mm; silt, with particles smaller than 0.02mm and larger than 0.002mm, and clay, with particles smaller than 0.002mm, to the ultra-microscopic.

Between the mineral particles are spaces, making up the pore space of the soil. The coarser particles—stones, gravel, sands and silt—are angular or rounded, relatively inert, and separately identifiable by feel and sight; and have relatively large pores to match. Water and air move through their mass freely. The finer particles of clay are quite different, being flattish and plate-like, lying closely together, and sticking when wetted so that the smallest of them are colloidal (glue-like). The spaces between clay particles are very small, holding water tenaciously, and resisting air-penetration; though the total pore space of a given mass of clay is greater than that of sand or silt.

Soils are classified according to the group of particles which are predominant in their make-up, which in turn establishes their physical texture or mechanical condition. Those with 80 per cent or more by weight of coarse particles are termed light, being open-textured, loose, and large-pored. Those with 30 per cent or more of the fine particles of clay are dense, sticky when wet, lumpy when dry, and are termed heavy. Between the two extremes, leavened by a better balance of particles, come the loams, ranging from the light loams in which sand and/or silt is dominant, through the desirable medium loams in which particles of all sizes are well balanced, to the heavy loams in which clay is an important factor.

ORGANIC CONTENT

Purely mineral soils are not fertile. They need an organic content to be able to nurture plants. This comes from the dead remains of plants, fungi, animals and micro-organisms accumulating in the soil. These are oxidized and broken down at variable rates by a myriad of soil organisms into small and smaller particles, with a release of the mineral elements originally taken up by the plant or animal, and the formation of a substance called humus.

Humus is difficult to define precisely, but is usually described as the brownish or blackish amorphous, jelly-like substance, largely composed of microscopic colloidal particles, formed in the decomposition of organic matter in the soil. It is one of the key life substances.

Being colloidal, it absorbs and holds moisture and soluble minerals tenaciously. Being sponge-like, it has a low density and relatively large air spaces, conducive to root penetration and activity. Physically, it gives a soil structure; filling-in the larger pores of sand, and slowing down water movement, while combining with the tiny fragments of clay to form granules or crumbs which then act like larger soil particles, with larger pores, and thus facilitating drainage and aeration. As it decays, organic matter darkens a soil, and it can then absorb and retain the sun's heat and energy more completely.

Humus functions as the centre of chemical ionic exchange and biological activities which transform the elements released from the organic matter- and from the inorganic mineral matrix of the soil into nutrients that plants eagerly take up for their growth and healthy function.

The first step in knowing your soil is to find out its type and basic physical characteristics. Start by examining when it is neither over-wet or over-dry, but moist, checking the top two to three inches. It should fall into one of the following categories.

Stony and gravel soils Usually recognisable on sight. Likely to drain freely, dry out very quickly in drought, and be difficult to work. But stones remain moist underneath, give cool root-runs to plants, although warming up quickly in the sun and sponsoring early growth. Large cumbersome stones are best removed; digging or forking in depth avoided; and the soil improved by top-dressings. Softish, sharp angular stones, sandstone, shale or limestone, break down more readily than rounded hard pebbles, and flints are best removed. Much depends upon the nature and sizes of the finer soil particles with the stones. Sift out and examine to check whether predominantly sandy, silty or clayey.

Sandy Soils   Dribble through readily when rubbed between the fingers and thumb, and feel grainy and gritty; a compressed handful fails to hold its shape when released. Loose, porous, easily worked at all times, absorbing sun and rain readily, but draining freely and soon drying out, with loss of soluble plant nutrients. Organic matter oxidizes quickly. Usually light in colour and light to work, warming up well for early growth. Do not need deep digging; best amended by top-dressing and enriching the near-surface soil, with plants responding to watering and foliar or liquid feeding in growth.

Silty Soils   When rubbed through the fingers and thumb silt has a less silky feel, less gritty than sand, and a compressed handful breaks down more slowly. More compact in settling, but resembles sandy soils to a lesser degree in character, and require similar treatment. If clay is present, however, the soil is likely to exhibit more of clay soil's qualities (q.v.); though it is not so sticky.

Clay Soils   Leave the fingers and thumb smeared when rubbed through them, feel sticky, and when compressed in the hand, remain a moulded lump, though the greater the amount of clay present, the more these characteristics show. Hold moisture well, tending to become waterlogged in wet periods, cracking and forming clods in dry, and are heavy to work, cold and slow to warm and therefore late in sponsoring plant growth in spring; but much richer in plant nutrients than sands.

Loam Soils   Range from sandy loams which are light and have good porosity, rubbing rather grittily through fingers and thumb, with a touch of silkiness and slight smearing, and forming a crumbly ball when compressed; through silty loams which are more puddingy, silky in feel, and compress more compactly; to clay loams which are heavy, especially when wet, leave well-smeared fingers and thumb when rubbed through, and form into balls of soil when compressed, though exhibiting a crumby structure when broken in two. Loams have all the good points of their components, and to a much smaller extent, their disadvantages; and hold moisture and plant nutrients accordingly.

Poppies are easy to grow and will brighten any garden

There are three other types of soil on which gardens have often to be made:

Calcareous Soils   These are soils overlying chalk or limestone rock, often shallow. The immediate topsoil may be sandy and light, quick-draining, porous, well-aerated and poor in plant nutrients and need handling as such. Any significant content of clay will make it heavier, more retentive of moisture and nutrients, though much stickier when wet. Chalk is simply a softer, more porous version of limestone; both are forms of calcium carbonate, which tends to make their soils alkaline, and restrictive in the range of plants which grow well in them.

Peat Soils   Often called bog, muck or fen soils, which are usually found in flat or low-lying areas, where plant remains have accumulated over aeons of time to form peat, though often mixed with fine sand, and silt, occasionally some clay. They vary from sandy heath land, to the soft muck land of old lakes or river beds, and moorland or mountain bog. The high organic content makes them spongy in character, moisture-retentive, usually strongly acid, but easily worked, though tending to shrink and pack down when drained.

Reclaimed Soils   Many gardens today have to be made on reclaimed ground, sometimes on ground where the surface soil has been removed, and a less fertile under- or sub-soil left. In other places, soil of indifferent quality has been used to fill in; and in others waste materials, municipal rubbish or industrial tip material has been used to make up a flat building site. All these are poor rooting mediums for plants. They need to be assessed for their physical properties such as porosity, drainage and aeration, and amended as required; and then it is most helpful to import a good loam topsoil to cover 10–15cm/4–6in deep, or at least fill pockets with such soil as planting stations for what we wish to grow.

A Simple Soil Analysis   To find out the physical composition of your soil you can take a typical sample of, say, two table-spoonfuls, place in a measuring cylinder or glass jar, add ten times as much water by volume, shake thoroughly, and allow to settle. The mineral particles will settle according to their surface area and density in more or less distinct layers—stones at the bottom, then smaller stones, coarse sand, fine sand, silt and clay, and by carefully measuring the layer thicknesses you can calculate their proportions.

Some of the finer particles of clay will remain suspended in the water, however, while at the top will float the organic matter and humus content. The more cloudy the water, the more colloidal particles are present in the soil. Your findings should confirm which type of soil you have, and give a fair indication of its humus resources. Ideally, the humus and organic matter should be 10–12 per cent at least by volume in proportion to the inorganic mineral particles.

The Importance of Drainage   The next thing you must know is how water behaves in your soil. Every soil has a certain capacity for water, like a sponge, but when there is an excess, it drives out the air, slows down or stops beneficial soil activities, and root function, disperses plant nutrients, and increases acidity. This can arise from rain not percolating through the soil readily, or from water moving from higher ground on or below the surface.

Dig holes about $60cm^2/2ft^2$ and 60–100cm/24–40in deep at the lowest levels of the site and watch how soil water behaves in them, after rain. If the water level or table rises short of the top 40cm/16in or so of soil, and goes down steadily after the rain has stopped, natural drainage is adequate. If it rises high, falls only slowly or remains long in winter, drainage is poor and needs attention. Rapid rise and swift fall, however, indicates that drainage is too free.

Where the topsoil becomes easily soaked and water forms puddles on the surface, you can break it up by cultivation, and condition it to a more permeable structure. Where the water table in the soil remains relatively high most of the time, drainage of the underlying soil is usually necessary, so that the water seeping in from surrounding ground may be dispersed.

Small areas or strips can be effectively improved by making holes in them, 1½–2m/5–6½ft deep, 2m/6½ft apart, with a posthole digger, and filling them to within 35cm/14in of the surface with broken rubble, stones, bricks or clinker, covered with an inverted sod, bark fibre, or peat, and then topsoil. Or a low-lying pocket to which soil water naturally seeps can be made into a water garden, with pool and bog.

Large areas need a grid of permeable clay or plastic drain tiles or drains, laid at 27–33cm/11–13in deep, 2–3m/6½–10ft apart, with a fall of 1 in 150 to 200, to the lowest point where there must be an outlet to a ditch, area drainage system, or a large soakaway or pit, 1–1.5m²/40–60in², and 1.5–2m/ 60–80in deep, filled with rubble, hard-core, broken stone or clinker to within 60cm/24in of the surface, and topped with inverted turf, wood shavings, peat or bark fibre, and topsoil.

Soil Acidity To know how acid (or alkaline) your soil is can be most helpful. It vitally affects the activity of beneficial organisms in the soil, influences the release of nutrient elements in quantity and kind to plant roots, and plays a part in the incidence of certain soil borne diseases and pests.

Soil acidity is measured by ascertaining the concentration of hydrogen ions (H) formed from acids, over that of hydroxyl ions (OH) formed from alkalines or bases, in the soil solution, and expressing it by a scale known as the pH scale or value. pH7 represents neutrality; lower values acidity, increasing in geometrical progression (pH6 is 10 times, pH5 100 times more acid than pH7); higher values alkalinity.

Most plants grow best in mildly acid to neutral soils (pH6–7); with some exceptions, but neither high acidity nor high alkalinity is well tolerated by garden plants. As the soil acidity changes and is not constant, checks should be run on the pH value from time to time, and selectively, having in mind the pH tolerances within which specific crops or plants grow best.

Soil acidity and pH value can be measured precisely with electrical equipment, but more simply and accurately enough for garden purposes by using a small soil-testing outfit* or soil-test litmus paper† which register the soil's reaction to coloured indicators.

*BDH Soil-Testing Outfit; Sudbury Lime Tester
†PBI Soil-test paper

Take a small sample of typical topsoil, treat it with the test fluid or paper, and note the colorometric response. Red (below pH5) indicates very strong acidity; orange to yellow (pH5.2–6), strong to medium acidity; yellow-green (pH6.2–6.5), mild to slight acidity; green (pH7) neutral acidity; greeny blue (pH7.2–7.5), mild alkalinity; and blue (pH7.6–8), increasing alkalinity.

Soil acidity responds to and is corrected by adding lime. It is much easier to reduce acidity than alkalinity. How much lime to use depends upon (a) the degree of acidity to be neutralised; (b) the kind of soil as lighter soils respond more quickly than heavy; (c) the kind of lime used.

Present pH value	Acidity rating	**Amount of hydrated lime needed to establish slight acidity of about pH6.5 in the following soils, per sq m/sq yd.**				
		Heavy clay or peat	Clay loams	Medium loams	Sandy loams or Silt	Light sand
4.5	extreme	500g/17oz	430g/15oz	370g/13oz	305g/10oz	245g/8oz
5.0	very strong	430g/15oz	370g/13oz	305g/10oz	245g/8oz	200g/6½oz
5.5	strong	370g/13oz	305g/10oz	245g/8oz	210g/7oz	180g/6oz
6.0	moderate	305g/10oz	210g/7oz	200g/6½oz	180g/6oz	165g/5½oz

Lime is best added separately. Mixed prematurely with manures or nitrogenous fertilizers it causes a loss of nutrients. Do it in autumn or early winter, after digging or organic manuring, by spreading evenly on the soil surface to be weathered in, at least six weeks before sowing or planting. Under cultivation, soils lose lime gradually, and dressings should be renewed every third or fourth year.

Plants differ in the amount of soil acidity they like best, and therefore in their need of lime, as the chart shows. A fair number of plants dislike or are intolerant of lime in the soil, and it is very difficult to change a soil of high pH value to suit them. The most acidifying agents are powdered sulphur and aluminium sulphate, but they act slowly, can do harm if over-applied, and are relatively expensive.

If you must grow lime-intolerant plants in a limy soil, remove the topsoil of a plant-station, dust the planting hole and sides with powdered sulphur (120g per m^2/4oz per yd^2), replace up to two-thirds the bulk of the topsoil with acid sphagnum moss peat or oak leaf-mould, and plant in this, adding a lacing of aluminium sulphate; about 60g per m^2/ 2oz per yd^2. Acid-reacting feeds, and the use of chelated foliar nutrients, will then help to keep the plants in good health.

The Soil Conditioners Soil conditioning is the business of amending the worst properties of its physical texture, and giving a structure that improves porosity to the advantage of good plant growth. The best soil conditioner for all mineral soils is humus-forming organic matter, but it is a bit slow, and its gradual effect can be enhanced by the use of soil-conditioning concentrates. The most effective are ground horticultural gypsum and seaweed derivatives.

Gypsum (calcium sulphate) works by displacing the elements, especially sodium, that make a soil sticky and heavy to work, and is therefore good for clay soils in particular. It does not alter soil acidity. Applied at 270–810g per m^2/9–28oz per yd^2, according to the clay in the soil, it results in better workability within a few weeks. It is best applied in the autumn or winter, and can be combined with lime if needed.

Seaweed decomposes to a jelly-like mass, containing many fine organic particles and substances known as alginates which help to make a better structure in all soils, particularly sandy and light ones. They can be used as powdered seaweed manure in autumn and winter, or in special formulations devised for soil conditioning, at 135–270g per m^2/$4\frac{1}{2}$–9oz per yd^2.

THE HUMUS FORMERS

The inorganic mineral mass of rock particles needs humus-forming organic matter to become living fertile soil. As the organic content of a soil diminishes in cultivation, it needs regular renewal. The more mineral the soil, the less fertile it is, and the more organic material it needs. Good humus formers are:

Animal manures from farmyard, stable, piggery and poultry house were once the mainstay of fertility, since they not only provided humus but useful amounts of plant nutrients, including nitrogen, potash and phosphorus. Traditionally, farmyard, and pig manure was used for light, sandy soils; stable manure for heavy; but all animal manures are good for all soils when they come from healthy animals and are properly used.

Manures should only be added fresh to soils that are vacant of plants and where they can have time to decay, usually in autumn. It is better to stack them, covered by a sprinkling of soil and a tent of sacking or sheet polythene, to pre-rot them for several weeks before use. Then they can be added to soils during the winter and early spring months. This practice should be followed particularly with strawy manure, or poultry manure from deep litter houses, where the bedding material is of sawdust, wood shavings or similar fibrous material. Such materials can be used at 25–50kg per m^2/$\frac{1}{2}$–1cwt per yd^2.

Garden compost can be a useful and regular source of humus. It consists of the organic waste materials and plant remains from garden and household. Anything of organic nature goes, except diseased plants, tough perennial weed roots, and large woody shoots and branches, plastic material, glossy paper, and synthetic man-made textiles.

Stack it in 10–20cm/4–8in layers, mixing coarse and fine material as much as possible, nicely moist but not saturated, firmed but not packed down air-tight, then dress with an activator which stimulates bacterial decomposition. The simplest activator is an inch or so of animal manure, plus a sprinking of topsoil and dusting of lime, and repeating the sequence until the heap is complete.

Compost should be made on the soil, not on impervious surfaces such as concrete. Proprietary activators should be used to the maker's instructions, and fall into two groups—organic (Q.R. Herbal Compost Maker; Bio, Maxicrop and seaweed powders); and chemical (Garotta, Comprot, Nitro-chalk, or nitrogenous fertilizers).

It is more efficient and tidier to make compost in containers or bins, which may consist of open wooden boxes, with slatted sides; netting enclosures of 2.5–5cm/1–2in mesh; plastic bags, well-holed for aeration, on wood or metal supports; or proprietary rigid plastic containers (Rotocrop). You need two so that compost can be made the year round, one maturing, and the other being built. Decomposition takes about 10 to 16 weeks, according to method, temperatures and season.

Once made a compost heap should be protected from soaking rains, and hard weather with a top cover of sacking, plastic sheeting or tarpaulin. Turning, shaking out and re-stacking, top to bottom, sides to middle, after the initial heating and shrinking of the heap, at 3-4 weeks, quickens decomposition and gives a more uniform end product. It is ready for use to manure, mulch or top-dress the soil when it becomes brown, easily broken up, pleasant smelling, and its ingredients are no longer separately recognisable.

Peat is best described as the organic remains of plants, accumulated under wet conditions over very many years, in an arrested state of decomposition. There are two kinds usually available, named according to the chief plants in their formation—sedge peats, and sphagnum moss peats. Sedge peats are less acid, and slightly less persistent in amending soils, but both are good humus formers and moisture retainers; clean and easy to handle. Excavated from natural deposits, air-dried, and then milled to various grades of fragmentation to suit various garden needs, they are available for immediate use under various brand names (Boothby, Alexander, Camelot, Golden Hornet, Fison's, LandP, Shamrock, Whiteheather, etc), though for manuring, coarser grades are best applied in autumn/winter months. They also need to be applied moist.

Peats are not rich in plant nutrients. Some peats can be obtained enriched with added nutrients (Bio-humus, Claverings, etc). Otherwise, peats need balanced compound fertilizers to complement them.

Bark fibre Pulverised and ground tree bark is a cheaper alternative to peat, slightly less acid, but poor in plant nutrients and less retentive of moisture (see Vita Bark, Forest Bark for brands). Pulverised bark amends light and sandy soils and is persistent, but use in autumn or winter. Ground bark makes a useful mulch. Both need the complement of balanced fertilizers with a rather high nitrogen content.

Leaf-mould   The leaves of beech, oak, hornbeam and similar thin leaves, decomposed in heaps for two to three years, are excellent moisture-holding, humus-forming materials, long-esteemed by gardeners, and can be used instead of, or to supplement other organic humus formers.

Hop manure   Spent hops from the brewery, with their flaky, easily rotted nature, make good humus, and can be used as an autumnal or winter manure. With balanced fertilizers added, they are sold as hop manure (Maskells, PBI) as a complete balanced feed for most garden plants.

Sewage sludge and **Municipal wastes**   Many public authorities now have the sense to process their sewage and refuse wastes into dried, milled and useful humus-forming material for gardens. Provided they are free of harmful industrial chemical waste, they make cheap organic improvers of soils, and reputable authorities supply their analysis, as to organic content, and chemical nature.

DIGGING TO A PURPOSE

Whether you do it by hand-digging and forking, or machine ploughing or rotavation, soil cultivation has a three-fold purpose: the control of weeds, by removal or burial; the making of better rooting quarters for garden seeds and plants by breaking-up the soil to help the movement of air and water; and the easy working-in of manures and fertilizers.

Digging or forking (a fork is easier to use on clay or heavy soils) is best done in the autumn/winter months, when the soil can lie exposed to further fragmenting by frost, wind and weather. The nearer the surface, the more fertile a soil is, since this is where the organic humus content is greatest and air and water move most freely, and bacterial and micro-organic life are most active. This is called the topsoil. Lower down the soil becomes progressively less fertile, more mineral, and less aerated and well drained. This is the subsoil. There is normally no clear demarcation, however. One of the main aims of gardening is to extend soil fertility in depth, and digging is a key method.

For convenience, soil depth is measured in spits. A spit is the depth to which a spade blade can be thrust. Simple digging means turning the soil one spit deep. On light, sandy, and easily worked soils which are naturally well drained, this is all that is needed. On heavy soils, sticky clays and where the soil beneath the top spit is panned hard, or impervious or solid like chalk, it is beneficial to dig deeper, turning the soil by the methods of double-digging or bastard-trenching.

Light, easily worked soils can be dug at convenience. With heavier soils the best times are when they are just drying out after rain, and are neither too sticky and wet, nor too hard and dry to work. Any green plant growth or grass sod can be stripped off thinly and either inverted at the base of the digging trench and dressed lightly with a sprinkling of a nitrogenous fertilizer (ammonium sulphate on chalk; nitro-chalk on acid soils) before turning the top spit over it; or stacked compactly, lightly dressed between every 15cm/6in with the chosen fertilizer, and covered with sheet polythene for 6 to 12 months, when it will form a crumbly loam, useful for top-dressings, or compost-making.

To dig a plot take out a trench of soil 30cm/12in wide, one spit deep, placing this soil where it will be needed to fill in the final trench of the plot at the opposite end; or by digging up one half of a plot and down the other half, transporting of the soil is minimised. The trench gives you elbow-room. In simple digging, the next 30cm/12in of soil is turned on to the exposed subsoil or second spit, and the sequence repeated. In double-digging, the second spit is forked over or broken up by pick-axe or mattock before turning the top spit on to it. Both spits must be kept at their own depths, not interchanged. The worked soil should then have time, at least four weeks, to settle and become integrated again before being sown or planted.

Fertilizers Feed Plants   The basic reason for adding fertilizers to garden soils is to provide nutrients for plant growth and health. They react with the soil to release nutrient elements as soluble inorganic mineral salts which enter the soil solution and from which they can be taken up by plant roots. Many are readily soluble and quick-acting, and therefore best used just before sowing or planting or to feed growing plants. Others break down less readily, and are slow- or steady-acting, tending to persist for some time. They are best used in autumn or winter ahead of the growing season.

Fertilizers are concentrated sources of the nutrient mineral elements that plants need for food. Properly used, they complement organic manuring in providing a balanced diet for plants. They make good the losses incurred in intensive garden cultivation, and can correct inherent deficiencies in a soil.

Of the major nutrients, fertilizers are usually compounded to supply nitrogen (N), phosphorus (P or P_2O_5) and potassium or potash (K or K_2O), the NPK trio. Of other macro-nutrients, calcium is supplied by liming; sulphur is rarely deficient in soils and occurs in many fertilizers as sulphate; magnesium and iron deficiencies are somewhat specialised, and may be easily corrected separately.

The micro-nutrients or trace elements which are only needed in very minute amounts are unlikely to be missing in any soil kept rich in humus by organic manuring. Those essential to plant growth, such as manganese, molydenum, boron, zinc, copper, can, however, be provided in the form of frits, formulated in special slowly soluble specks of glass, and are likely to be most beneficial on poor mineral soils, subsoils and reclaimed soils being brought into cultivation.

Organic v Inorganic Fertilizers Organic fertilizers are concentrates from plant or animal remains. They have to be decomposed in the soil before their nutrients are released. This takes time. With one exception—dried blood—they are slow-acting and effective for more than one growing season. By their nature they are slightly humus-forming, contain tiny amounts of other elements than the major one they supply, and nurture and stimulate soil micro-organisms. They are safe in the sense that overdoses do not harm; but comparatively expensive. Nurserymen like them because they release a steady supply of nutrients over a long period, and with regular use build up a reserve of fertility in the soil.

Excepting dried blood and seaweed extracts which are readily soluble and best used to feed plants in the growing season, the organic fertilizers should be applied in autumn or early winter. They make excellent soil dressings for autumn–winter planted shrubs, trees, and perennial stock—hoof and horn meal for nitrogen, bone meal for phosphorus, and powdered seaweed for potash.

Inorganic fertilizers, called artificials or more irreverently 'bag muck', are chemical salts; manufactured, synthesised or derived from natural mineral deposits. Readily soluble and therefore quick-acting, they are most effectively and economically used in late winter, spring and early summer when plants are in their active phases of growth.

They need to be used with some precision, since overdoses not only unbalance nutrition and plant growth but adversely affect soil chemistry and structure.

Fertilizers may be used to provide only one mineral nutrient, and as such are referred to as straight fertilizers, to be used singly to meet a definite nutritional need or soil deficiency, or more preferably in combination, balanced to feed plants more completely.

APPLYING FERTILIZERS

Fertilizers are offered in powdered, fine crystals, or granular form for dry application, and as such should be applied to moist soil, after or before rain, or be watered in so that they dissolve readily. They are also prepared in liquid concentration for dilution and application by watering can or sprayer, for use in the growing season. Recommended dosage should be followed. It is wasteful and possibly harmful to over-apply. Unless stated to be safe for foliar (leaf) application, fertilizers are best applied to the soil without touching the plants.

Fertilizer application falls into three phases:

Autumn/Winter   when the slow-acting fertilizers are applied —hoof and horn meal, slow-release nitrogen, bonemeal, seaweed powder, basic slag, and on light soils potassic salts such as kainit.

Late Winter/Early Spring   when base compound fertilizers are applied, prior to sowing or planting, to meet the nutritional needs of plants for the growing season. They provide nitrogen, phosphorus, and potash balanced to meet the needs of what is grown. They can be made up at home from straight fertilizers but require skilful and careful mixing. Most gardeners and nurserymen find it simpler and more efficient to use factory-mixed and formulated compounds, which are usually in granular form to give a more even release of nutrients.

The packages indicate the strength of their contents in three figures, such as 5:7:9, meaning 5 per cent nitrogen, 7 per cent phosphorus, 9 per cent potash, always in that order. Some makers add other nutrients such as magnesium and trace elements which is all to the good. Mixtures may be purely chemical, part chemical, part organic, or purely of organic materials, and there is a wide range of choice.

A straightforward plan is to use a general compound which can be applied safely to all plants—vegetables, flowers, ornamental trees and shrubs and fruit crops—simply varying the rate of application. 'Growmore'—7:7:7—sponsored by the Ministry of Agriculture originally, is an inorganic chemical mixture; John Innes Base—5.1:6.4:9.7—is a chemical and organic mix; and seaweed with dried blood or prepared seaweed products are purely organic base fertilizers.

Specially formulated mixtures can then be used for specific crops such as tomatoes, or favourites such as roses, chrysan-themums, sweet peas, and lawns for better-than-average performance and yields.

Late Spring/Summer when plants are growing actively are the times to boost their performance or help them over setbacks caused by unfavourable weather, pests or disease with quick-acting feeds in suitably light applications. Many plants, particularly leafy greens, benefit from a nitrogenous application (sodium nitrate, dried blood, nitro-chalk) when just past the seedling stage, or a light application of a general fertilizer can be made, and watered in if the weather is dry.

It is more quickly effective to use dilute liquid feeds—liquid manure, prepared by steeping cow, horse or poultry manure in a barrel of water for 2–3 weeks, and drawing off the liquid to dilute it to a straw colour for use; chemical liquid concentrations, diluted with water; or organic liquid concentrations such as seaweed extracts and/or dried blood, suitably diluted.

In feeding with dry or liquid fertilizers, the application should be to the soil covering the rooting area, slightly wide of the base of plants. Feeds can be given at one to three week intervals up to flowering or fruiting but discontinued when plants reach seasonal maturity and the peak of the seasonal growing cycle has been passed.

Growing plants may also be fed through their leaves, and foliar feeding as it is called is an economical and very quick way of improving growth, as nutrients pass into the tissues for almost immediate use. Obviously, non-scorching benign solutions must be used, together with a wetting agent, either chemical or organic. The seaweed preparations seem particularly suited to this type of feeding, since they contain such a wide range of nutrients.

Foliar feeding is particularly valuable in meeting specific nutrient deficiencies, and formulations carrying chelated compounds of iron, manganese and magnesium are particularly useful in correcting chlorosis often exhibited by plants on calcareous soils. Foliar feeds can be repeated at 7–10 day intervals preferably in the early morning or evening of a dry day or when rain is not imminent.

3
Planning and Planting

Making a garden is a matter of reconciling dreams with reality. Before you plant, you must plan—in your mind's eye, or better still on paper. The location, latitude, aspect, exposure, soil, subsoil and relationship of your garden site to its surrounding environment are powerful factors in determining what plants you can grow well, and therefore the features of your layout.

Your Garden on Paper   Begin with a sheet of square-lined graph paper, mounted on hardboard, the bigger the better; on which you can line in your boundaries and buildings to scale. Add the compass bearing. Mark in permanent structures like power poles, manhole covers, existing shrubs and trees, and indicate any nearby buildings, structures or trees outside your boundaries likely to affect such matters as light, shade and wind behaviour in your garden area.

If the site is new to you, spend some time at different periods of the day observing the play of the elements on it. Note areas of shade and light. Mark slopes and their direction, and areas most exposed to prevailing winds and draughts, low-lying points which may be frost pockets, or lie wet after heavy rains, any problem areas of weed infestation, and not least the soil—kind, depth and underlying strata—all factors which will affect plants and how well they can grow for you.

Now you can decide where to place your garden services and furnishings: your potting shed, compost yard and bins, greenhouse and propagating frames, with access paths. For aesthetic reasons you will want to place them unobtrusively, but remember glass structures must have maximum light. Provision for a clothes line with firm access is usually necessary, and where there are children an area for play and a sand-pit may be needed.

Formal or Informal?   A formal garden laid out with symmetry and on geometrical lines will call for stonework in paving, terracing, walling and ornament, and can be made attractive by contrasting textural areas of large pebbles, cobblestones or gravel. Plant relief is afforded by beds or areas of greenery such as tailored lawns, ground cover plants, and beds of dwarf flowering shrubs, roses, perennials or bedding plants, and the selection of plants of some architectural habit such as shapely, columnar, fastigiate, pyramidal upright growth and horizontal or tiered growing shrubs and trees, particularly evergreens and conifers naturally neat and compact, or tameable by periodic trimming.

In such a garden large pots, tubs and vases can be used for growing choice plants, esteemed for their foliage and flowering merits, and allowing for changes to be rung by their very mobility. Seasonal flowers, such as annuals, bulbs, dahlias, 'geraniums' and plants of doubtful hardiness can be grown in such containers, and as the soil mixture can be pre-determined, plants alien to the native soil, such as camellias and rhododendrons, can be tub-grown. A pool, stocked with aquatic plants and goldfish, can be pleasingly incorporated in a formal design, provided it has an open situation.

In flagged or gravelled areas, planting stations may be left in which container-grown specimen plants can be set, and give instant effect. Changes can be easily rung by growing plants in plastic pots and burying these to their rims in such positions, to give of their seasonal best, and then replaced or changed around. After all changing the furniture in a room can refresh it, and the same intent can be achieved outdoors, by growing some plants in moveable containers.

Admittedly, the formal garden is expensive in first cost, but relatively easy to maintain. It is often a better solution for a small area than the pocket-handkerchief lawn and fringe borders, especially for gardens subject to shade and where the soil is poor or impoverished by invading roots of trees you have to accept. A possible disadvantage is that nature is less than devoted to formal lines and symmetry, and with neglect will undo them. The invasion of greenish growths of algae, lichen and moss unless repelled by periodic application of an algicide (Dimanin, Algofen, Fungo) to stone, often comes first, and there is a strong tendency to uneven or unequal development in plants chosen to match one another when growing apart due to slight variations in their environmental conditions.

Informality   This implies the free association of plants and garden features in some irregularity and blended disorder with the intent of realising the appeal of a textured and colourful landscape that is also restful and enchanting. Complete informality, bordering on the semi-wild with oases of disciplined features, calls for the space of the country. Modern gardens, of small dimensions, cheek by jowl with others, call for a compromise, and a sensible approach is to be formal and precise near to the house with terrace, patio or flagging and narrow borders and plants of narrow upright growth, such as climbers or tallish shrubs near the walls, and compact inmates for the borders. Merge this into a more informal and naturalistic layout the farther away from the house you go.

Sloping sites can be made more workable and attractive by splitting and levelling with low retaining walls and shallow steps, easier to maintain than bankings. To give the illusion of spaciousness to small gardens, the layout should aim for openness at the centre with vistas to be glimpsed from the doors and windows of the home leading to particular features and drawing the eye into exploration.

Garden Features   The choice of garden features will reflect your own tastes in what you wish to grow. Their success, however, will be governed by their practicality and suitability to the conditions you have to offer, and the matter of upkeep is usually highly important.

A rock garden for alpine plants can be big or small, constructed as a corner outcrop, a tor-like island or on the slopes of a valley formation; but basic essentials are a well-lighted aspect,

A well-trimmed lawn and neatly kept paths are essential to the final
appearance of a garden

perfect drainage, porous soil, sandy or gritty, with humus from leaf-mould or rotting peat, into which roots can penetrate deeply and readily, and of rocks well-embedded and suited to the needs of the plants to be grown. Limestone and tufa suits alpines of the Dolomites, but many plants from gneiss, granite, slate and sandstone areas are acid-lovers. Remember that rock gardens are weed catchers, for which manual control is largely needed, as chemicals must be used with caution.

There is little difficulty in establishing a pool and water garden, given an open site, in these days when prefabricated pool containers are so readily available in various shapes and sizes. Once stocked with a balance of underwater oxygenating plants, surface leafing and flowering water-lilies and the like, and marginal plants, a garden pool requires only an annual check-up and makes a labour-saving fascinating feature. A low-lying situation is often ideal, but an area which is permanently ill-drained and moist can be transformed by a pool or canal-like ditch, flanked by bog and semi-aquatic plants.

Rose Gardens   It is hard to pass the roses by, but few plants are more exacting. They need skilled pruning, careful and liberal feeding, much coddling against diseases and pests, are prickly, and look bare and forlorn for half the year, though their flowers are deserving of all the superlatives heaped upon them. For their healthy, robust culture, you must give them open conditions in the sun, a moisture and nutrient retentive well-drained soil of heavy texture, and the care of an enthusiast with knowledge and time to devote to their needs; then you can lay out chosen kinds and varieties in beds or borders, with perhaps underplantings of pansies, violas, myosotis and bulbs for relief.

Flower Beds and Borders   These can give colour from frost to frost. Annuals, grown from seeds, make for cheap, quick, and surprisingly long periods of colourful bloom. Helped by modern balanced fertilizers, they grow in most soils, and can be chosen to suit various situations, and aspects. There is, however, the expense of raising them anew each year and the labour of bedding them out in a busy spring to be met.

A mass of climbing roses can disguise unsightly garden buildings

Fine colour can also be provided by the half-hardy perennials, such as begonias, dahlias, 'geraniums', and fuchsias, at the cost of planting out each spring, lifting each autumn, and housing in frost-proof quarters each winter.

The well planned and planted herbaceous border of perennial flowering plants is a garden glory, but demands ample space, good sun, good soil, and much maintenance in staking, feeding, clearance of matured growth in autumn, and manuring. It is often easier to feature such plants in island beds or to grow selected robust kinds mixed with choice shrubs in a mixed planting that eases maintenance.

Shrubs when well chosen for their foliage, shapeliness, habit and flowers provide permanent attractions with low maintenance needs. To give of their best they need to be chosen for their hardiness, suitability for the position and soil where they are to grow, and with keen appreciation of their height, width and looks when mature. A well associated border or island group can be distinctive the year round.

Heathers and heaths lend themselves to long-blooming colourful features, weed-containing and easily maintained. Most gardens can grow some of the lime-tolerant winter–spring flowering Ericas, but others, chiefly summer-flowering and the heathers or ling, need lime-free soil.

The Vegetable Plot   An area for vegetable-growing needs to be set apart, in full sun, where the soil has good potential for cultivation in depth, and preferably where a good rotation can be practised, with access both in tending it and harvesting crops. An area of 250–275m^2/275–300yd^2 is needed to feed a family of four well. A smaller area should be set aside for culinary herbs, for which the soil does not need to be rich, but well-drained and in the sun.

The Garden Orchard   Tree fruits, especially the stone fruits (peaches, gages, plums, cherries) and standard apples and pears need ample room. Apples and pears can be planted to make bush or pyramidal growth on dwarfing rootstocks where space is at a premium, and trained cordon or espalier trees lend themselves to line growing on wires, on walls, by paths, or as dividers between one part of a garden and another.

The bush fruits—black, red and white currants, and gooseberries—and the cane fruits—raspberries, blackberries, loganberries—fruit more consistently, more heavily, per square metre than the tree fruits and are excellent for small gardens. Strawberry beds usually have a life of four years before needing renewal, and can be placed in the vegetable plot quite happily.

Boundaries These may be of walls, fences or hedges. Solid walls and fences can be used for the support of climbing ornamental shrubs or fruiting brambles, vines, trained trees chosen for their suitability to the aspect. Good boundaries blunt wind, and within their lee, any border is sheltered, calm and usually a few degrees warmer than the open garden, and therefore a useful place for choice plants and early growth. Where they cast excessive shade, however, plants adapted to such conditions will have to be grown such as ferns, evergreens and plants native to the undergrowth of woods—Japanese anemones, foxgloves, doronicums, honesty, etc.

Wind, stopped by an obstacle, is forced upwards until it can move freely again, and descends with greater force and turbulence at about 10 to 12 times the height of the obstacle in distance. Because they tend to absorb some of the thrust of a wind, being permeable, hedges make the better windbreaks.

PLANTING

When the general layout and disposition of the special features is decided, some thought should be given to planting and factors influencing performance of plants. Obviously, the more soundly the soil is prepared, the more ready plants will be to grow and thrive. The emphasis should be on simplicity, concentrating on a few of the most desirable features than many, and planning their planting in groups of like plants rather than a multiplicity of single plants in an effort to grow as many species, hybrids and varieties as possible. Restraint will result in more striking effects.

The chief sowing season is March to June, although an earlier start can be made with heat under glass. The most critical factor in germination is soil temperature, though seeds must also have access to moisture and air. Plants can be grown from seeds throughout the warm months, and later summer and autumn sowings of biennials and hardy annuals may often be made, but the earlier the better for seedlings to over-winter.

Traditionally and rightly the planting season for leaf-losing deciduous shrubs, trees and herbaceous perennials extends from leaf-fall in autumn to bud-swelling in spring. For evergreens and conifers which have no dormancy, it is either late September to November *or* late March to May. Do not be tempted to set out such plants in the cold or wet winter weeks, although they are offered freely enough. Some plants, notoriously difficult to transplant, such as brooms, magnolias, pampas grass, are best planted in April–May.

Increasingly, many plants are now grown in containers from which they can be planted with little or no disturbance of their roots. As quite sizeable plants are obtainable in this way, garden effects and scenes can be created almost instantly at almost any time of the year. But check that the plant has not been too long in its container with the development of a congested and bound root system—or too short, when recovery will be erratic. In planting, make the soil rich enough to excite new root growth into it, keep moist in dry weather, and syringe the foliage often after planting on hot days.

Hardiness In choosing outdoor plants go for hardiness or ability to thrive under the climatic conditions you have. Bear in mind the farther north you are, the later your spring, and the earlier your autumn, and again that the western watersheds and coasts of Britain are kinder to plants of the warmer temperate zones than the eastern. Plants can only prosper in conditions approximate to those of their native habitat.

At the same time, a garden can modify local weather conditions as it becomes established and pockets or areas of greater warmth and shelter from wind and cold air currents are created by plants, with the taller shielding the shorter, while plant cover itself helps to mitigate the effects of prolonged dry weather, and the too rapid loss of heat and moisture. It often becomes possible to grow plants of less hardiness that would not survive under bare exposure.

Plants and Soils   At the outset it is wise to choose plants for the soil in which they are to grow. The big divide is between plants which are tolerant of lime and the intolerant. The latter are the fewer, chiefly genera of the *Ericaceae* or Heath family, with a few exceptions. Other plants with a low lime-tolerance include *Camellia, Eucryphia, Halesia, Kalmia, Ledum, Lithospermum prostratum, Magnolia, Pieris*, autumn-flowering gentians, and alpines of high moors and granite mountains.

Given a definitely alkaline chalky or limy soil, it is sensible to plant species from calcareous habitats until the soil can be changed. Most plants and crops are happy in soils containing lime but acid in reaction. Care will be needed, however, in selecting plants for quick-draining soils that dry out rapidly, and poorly drained soils that remain wet or waterlogged long, until physical conditions are improved. On poor soils, lacking humus, leguminous trees, shrubs and plants should be given priority—genera of the *Leguminosae* or *Papilionaceae*—which have a symbiotic association with the root nodule bacteria to fix nitrogen from the air.

Light and Shade   Broadly, plants need sun to flower well, and it is the shaded parts of the garden that call for the more specialised shade-tolerant plants, though with their rich green, often tough and leathery leaves, or much divided foliage, they tend to bear only small, whitish or greenish flowers. The most difficult places to populate are those of deep persistent shade in the lee of buildings or walls, where ferns, mosses, ivies and evergreens can survive; in the dappled shade of trees or of deciduous trees, plants which flower in the first months of the year are the most likely to succeed.

Wind and Plants   Wind is the worst weather enemy of plants. It accentuates the effects of other prevailing conditions, making heat more desiccating, cold more chilling, and rain more damaging than when the air is still. Near the coast, on-shore winds may carry sea salt to blacken and kill foliage. Wind can pick up dust, sand and atmospheric pollution with which to hammer plants. Wind funnelling down alleys, or whipping round corners can be like a tornado to plants. None are wind-proof, though the grey-leafed and the spiny often survive well. Initial shelter is best provided by permeable fencing, such as trellis, peastick hedging, chestnut paling, netted plastic sheeting, honeycomb brick or concrete work, to permit plants to become established in their lee. Only in wider settings is it possible to establish plant windbreaks or shelter belts of shrubs or trees in depth.

Height and Spread   Taking account of how tall a plant can grow and how wide it will spread when full-grown can avoid the grief of having to cut down a noble specimen grown too big for its surroundings, and save much labour and time in trying to make others fit restricted space. Forest trees are ill-suited to small gardens, and to avoid damage by their roots undermining the house, it is essential to plant trees with a spreading head at least as far away as their potential height, for root spreads tends to exceed branch spread in most species.

Height and spread should be kept well in mind when choosing and planting shrubs, small trees and other plants. Young plants look puny when first planted, and the temptation to plant closely must be resisted, since, later on growth that has to be curtailed presents problems. Better to in-fill with annuals or quick-growing plants such as santolinas, lavenders, etc, which can be sacrificed without heartbreak.

4

Planning the Open Spaces

Your garden will always give you delight when you can look at and into it, your eye moving to pleasing vistas along open pathways, and into spaces flanked and contained by plantings attractive for their colour, and display of plant habit and form.

Paths and flat open areas such as patios and terraces are important skeletal parts of garden design to be made early in laying out the landscape. They are essentially functional, to give access; but laid in harmonious materials and rightly planned, they merge unobtrusively with the scene, and provide safe and agreeable hard footing in all weathers.

Approach paths from highway to house and service paths to greenhouse or compost yard usually need to be straight, direct and as short as practicable. Within the garden they may serve practical and aesthetic ends. A path at the foot of a terrace or low wall, or bordering a bed of flowers or shrubs may make tending as well as viewing easier. Flags, arranged like stepping stones, in a lawn, are often useful and contrast with the green. They do not need to be rectangular, but can be oval or round or of even less conventional shape, provided they are placed at well-measured strides apart.

Paths within the garden are more inviting when they meander, but should have point, either leading to a terminal point such as the rock garden, a seat, an arbour, a sundial or piece of statuary, or a place to pause and contemplate a new vista such as a rose garden or glade.

A patio or terrace, usually approached by french windows or door from the house, is a large path, and provides a place to relax, and enjoy outdoor meals in the warmer months, if at least $2\frac{1}{2}$m/8ft wide.

PATH MAKING

Straight paths can be marked out with string and two sticks or a garden line; curved or serpentine paths with a length or two of hosepipe. Those which need to take a barrow or machines should be at least 110cm/44in wide, but less hardly used paths may be 61–76cm/24–30in wide. After removing soil to a depth suitable to take the path and its foundations, levelling is done by (a) driving in square pegs to the finished height of the path, at least three equidistant apart; (b) standing tee-shaped flat wooden crosses, called boning rods, of similar size, say 1m/3ft tall, on two end-pegs, and with a third boning rod on intermediate pegs, check the levels by sighting with the eyes across the tops of the tee pieces; adjusting the heights of the intermediate pegs until all are level.

Permanent paths need adequate foundations, the depth of which will vary according to the paving material used, and the weight of traffic. When stone flags, concrete slabs, bricks, crazy paving or wood blocks are to be used a foundation of hardcore (packed broken stone, brick, clinker, rubble, etc) is needed to make the soil firm, topped by a 3–6cm/1–2in thick layer of ashes, setting sand or fine dry soil, tamped or rolled firm, before laying the chosen path material with the help of cement mortar.

On patios, forecourts and much-used paths, flags or slabs are best laid in a 2.5cm/1in layer of mortar (1 part by volume Portland cement, 2 parts damp sand, 3 parts aggregate, and approximately $\frac{3}{4}$ part water); otherwise, it is usually sufficient to trowel small heaps of mortar at each corner of a flag or slab, and position and level it; using a straight-edge (15cm/6in wood board on edge, with spirit-level).

Interstices may be filled in and pointed with cement mortar, with open spaces left where you want to place plants. In laying crazy paving, the outside edges must be straight and parallel, and the largest pieces placed down the centre, close enough not to trap heels. Bricks should be the hard, well-burnt seconds or rejects of the kiln. Wooden blocks, laid with the grain vertical, can be set on sand, with a coating of bitumen between them, or be treated with preservative beforehand (Cuprinol, Horticel, Presotim, Solignum) for long life.

LAWNS – MAKING AND MAINTAINING

Grass lawns make the most popular covering for garden space but are relatively costly features to establish and maintain. The site must be very thoroughly prepared, to give first-class drainage, good topsoil porosity, adequate humus from actively rotting organic matter, a soil acidity below pH6.5, and freedom from perennial weeds and their roots; and must be open.

Lawn grasses are adapted meadow or pasture grasses. None are truly dwarf-growing, though some grow less tall and strains of slower growth are now available. Inescapably, a lawn needs a cutting machine, and the time and energy to use it frequently during the growing season.

Lawns from Turf Site and soil need the same meticulous preparation for the instant lawn possible by laying turf as for seeding. Turf is best laid from September to March in mild weather when the soil is workable. At other times, it will need nursing along, watering in dry periods, shading in heat, until rooting well. The big problem is suitable turf. There are few turf nurseries. Sea-washed or Cumberland turf is fine, but needs good culture, and does not always transplant well inland. Local turf from pastures, heathland, downland or parkland is often offered, and if de-weeded, and well cared for, makes a useful sward. Turf should be 30.5/12in wide, 30.5–100cm/12–40in long, and only about 2.5–3cm/1–1½in thick, for laying.

The sods are laid from one corner or one side, working forward, and in bonded formation like brickwork. Any unevenness is corrected by adding or removing soil underneath; each sod being lightly firmed into place, and the whole lawn dressed with coarse sand and brushed, and then topped with a thin layer of sifted compost or lawn peat. A light rolling and cutting in a week or so may follow.

Lawns from Seed Capital costs are less for a sown lawn. You can also ensure that you grow only the appropriate grasses from the start. But it takes longer for the sown lawn to be put to use. Sowing times are late summer (August–September) or early Spring (late March–May), if trying weather to hazard grass seedlings is to be avoided.

Lawns of bowling green or golf green quality call for seeds of Fescues (Chewing's Fescue, creeping Red Fescue S59) and Browntop Bent, in proportions adjusted to the soil, location and function.

For ornamental, less costly lawns smooth-stalked Meadow-grass may be included for dry light soils; rough-stalked Meadow-grass for heavy moist soils, crested dogstail for hard wear though not for fine swards, and Ryegrass S23 for leafiness and colour. Seedsmen, specialising in grasses, make up a variety of mixtures; and it is better to buy a properly blended mixture, treated with a bird and pest repellent, than to mix your own. Where a standard mixture will not suit, you can have one made up to suit the soil, location and climate of your garden.

Sowing technique calls for a light two-way raking of the firmed level site to leave it criss-crossed with shallow furrows; even distribution of the seed at 30–45g per m^2/1–1$\frac{1}{2}$oz per yd^2, by mixing the seed with twice its volume of sand, and sowing one half one way, the other crosswise. A light raking and firming to just cover and embed the seed is all that is then needed. Grass seeds germinate better in subdued light and do not need to be buried deeply. In autumn, germination takes 5–10 days; in spring up to twice as long.

When about 6cm/2$\frac{1}{2}$in high, a light rolling and cutting to reduce the grass by 3cm/1in can be done. Thereafter, cutting should be frequent, keeping pace with growth, but not close until well established.

Lawn maintenance   To keep a mono-culture feature such as a lawn in beautiful condition calls for more than mowing and rolling. Mowing should aim at keeping the grasses at a height suitable for the lawn's purpose—shaven for ball games, but longer at about 1.25–2cm/$\frac{1}{2}$–1in, for ornamental lawns. But cutting must be consistent, keeping pace with growth. The more often a lawn is cut when growing vigorously, the less total weight of foliage is removed, and the less strain on the growth energies and economy of the plants. And appearance remains good.

46

Rolling is needed to true the surface only. Superficial bumps and ridges should be levelled by stripping back the turf and adjusting the soil level beneath—not by heavy rolling. A roller mower is usually sufficient for garden purposes.

Aeration is the proper complementary treatment to mowing in maintaining a lively healthy sward. It stimulates healthy root action, and prevents the accumulation of dead organic matter and a matted turf. This can be done by using a simple turf slitting or spiking tool, manual or powered, each year, prior to applying fertilizers or top-dressings. Badly matted and compacted turf, especially on heavy soils, benefits by being forked with a tool fitted with hollow tines, removing small cores of turf and soil. At a push, the garden fork can be inserted and wiggled to leave holes at regular intervals.

Feeding This falls into two parts—top-dressing to improve the soil, fertilizing to feed the grass. On light soils a mixture of loam and sifted compost or lawn peat helps moist; on heavy soils coarse sand or powdered burnt earth should take the place of the loam; on loam soils just sand is usually sufficient. If the acidity of the soil falls below pH5, a dressing of basic slag, about 120g per m^2/4oz per yd^2 may be included. Where water-lodging and stagnancy occur, crushed charcoal is helpful.

Mowing removes mineral nutrients in the leaves to depress soil fertility. Fertilizing to make good this loss consists of an autumnal application of a mixture low in nitrogen, high in phosphates, moderate in potash, and an early spring balance of high nitrogen, with moderate readily available phosphates and potash—well catered for in the proprietary fertilizers offered by well-known firms. A simplified routine that meets the needs of plain garden lawns is: bonemeal at 60–80g per m^2/2–3oz per yd^2 with $12g/\frac{1}{2}$oz potassium sulphate in autumn, and a dressing of the St. Ives lawn fertilizer* at 60–80g per m^2/2–3oz per yd^2 in late March.

*15 parts by weight ammonium sulphate, 15 parts dried blood, 40 parts fine bonemeal, 25 parts superphosphate, 5 parts potassium sulphate

Weeding   Most broad-leaved weeds can be controlled by the use of selective herbicides which act by disrupting growth functions. They should be used when weeds are in active growth, preferably in May–June on a day when rain is not imminent for a general clearance; and thereafter to spot-treat recalcitrant plants. It is vital to match the herbicide to the weeds, and the makers' information should be studied. Daisies, plantains and similar rough-leaved weeds may be discouraged by applying lawn sand, a mixture of 3 parts by weight ammonium sulphate and 1 part ferrous sulphate, bulked with 15–20 parts of sand, to lightly coat the leaves. Weeds resistant to chemical control must be hand-weeded, and these include coarse grasses such as couch and Yorkshire fog.

Other Lawns   Chamomile (*Anthemis nobilis*) is a prostrating perennial with finely divided foliage sometimes used for lawns on poorish soils, in warm localities, grown from stem cuttings, preferably of a non-flowering strain, set 10–15cm/4–6in apart in weed-free soil in spring, needing only occasional cutting to keep it trim. In shade where grasses grow poorly, a cover of Ivies (*Hedera helix* and vars), or Periwinkles (*Vinca major*, *V. minor* and vars) are worth considering for no-trouble cover.

5
Tooling Up

Tools for gardening come in many kinds, sizes and shapes, and there are gadgets innumerable. Most of them are for seasonal or periodic use, and a sensible assessment before buying any tool is to ask yourself how many days it is likely to languish in the tool shed unused. It may be cheaper to hire a hedge trimmer or cultivator for the short time you need it.

One of the first tools to buy is a measuring tape in stainless spring steel or plastic-coated fibre glass, well marked metrically as well as in imperial. A collapsible one that can be carried in the pocket will often be used in marking out and designing your garden. To this I would add at least one marking stick which you will have to make yourself, using either a 12.5mm diameter dowel rod or strong wooden lath, painted with bright yellow polyurethane paint, with nicks for cm/in markings, lined with black paint. A metre-long stick is invaluable for the quick-spacing of beds, rows and plants in the vegetable plot and planting elsewhere.

TOOLS FOR SOIL CULTIVATION

Working the soil has the practical aims of admitting air and light, improving drainage and stimulating bio-chemical reactions. It facilitates the incorporation of soil improving materials such as manures, and fertilizers, and gives a surface finish that contrasts well with plants and pleases aesthetically. At the same time, too much cultivation can defeat these ends.

In choosing tools, assess them ergonomically—for their feel, size and weight, visualizing how well they will function as extensions of your body in carrying out their function. Quality is important, appearance less so, but a tool that is right will feel part of you as a gardener.

The **spade** comes first, the **fork** second. Choose for balance in your hands when held horizontally in front of your knees, and for easy penetration and release of the soil. The blades can be of stamped steel, forged steel or stainless steel—the first being the cheapest and least durable. In forged steel, the blade may be finished half-bright or all-bright, the latter being the easier to work, but both need scraping free of soil after use, and spraying or wiping with a rust-preventive oil after use, if they are to remain bright. In stainless steel, the extra initial cost is offset by easy-working, and rust-resistance. The cutting edge of a spade should be kept chisel sharp, and the tines of a fork well pointed.

Wooden handles, even in the best ash, tend to weaken in time, and need a good application of linseed oil occasionally. The newer plastic fibre handles are more resistant to neglect.

Sizes range from No. 1 for borders and ladies' use, through No. 2, probably the most useful for the garden, to the bigger No. 3 and 4 which are for professionals and strong men. Spade shapes may vary with a straight or rounded cutting edge, and may be obtained with a flange or tread on the top edge to protect your footwear, and handles can be tee-, dee-, y-shaped at the top, to personal preference.

The long-shafted spade with pointed blade, common in Asia, Europe and America, can be used with little back-bending and is worth considering where much soil has to be excavated or moved. The spring lever spade eases muscle work, as when the blade has been thrust into the soil, the release of the spring lever throws the spade load forward, but does not turn it or break it up.

A matching **fork** is needed to break up the soil, help to remove weeds and roots, to handle organic materials, to harvest root crops, to loosen and turn over clay and heavy soils and to turn compost heaps. A standard, straight-shanked fork with square sectioned tines will do all these operations; though on a clay soil a flat-tined fork for digging, may be considered; and a dished fork with round or oval tines would handle manure and compost better.

A **rake** is necessary to work surface soil to a fine tilth in preparing seed beds, and to incorporate surface dressings of lime or fertilizer. A steel-comb type with 12 oval or rounded pointed teeth and a long handle is most useful, though rakes with fewer or more teeth are available for restricted or open spaces. For the collecting of leaves, clearing up of rubbish, or the scarifying of lawns a 'Wizard' rubber-toothed straight rake or a fan-shaped, spring-toothed rake comes in very useful from time to time.

The **hoe** is chiefly used in the sowing and growing season. A triangular hoe is useful for making vee seed drills, though this can also be done by pushing the back of a rake into the soil along a garden line, or with a spade. A draw hoe, or swan-necked Bury hoe, with a half-rounded blade, is used to make wide shallow seed drills, and to chop out weeds, and earth up crops like potatoes.

In the growing season, a hoe may be used to control seedling weeds, and to prevent a sealed cap forming on soils after rain that would impair root aeration. For this, the Dutch hoe with a flat sharp blade is used, pushed shallowly through the top half-centimetre of soil to sever the weed stems and mix the remains with the soil. Variations are the push-pull and swoe hoes, with cutting edges on both sides of their blades. You can probably do without a weeding hoe if you use a paraquat/diquat contact herbicide to destroy young weeds.

Trowels are indispensable hand tools for planting-out, frame and greenhouse work, and from a number of varieties offered, a short handled, tang-type with round-pointed blade for general use, and a narrow-bladed kind with depth measurements marked for bulb planting are good basic buys, in forged or stainless steel for long life.

Hand forks for weeding and cultivating close to plants, the short-handled for close work, the long-handled for levering out stubborn well-rooted weeds. A fork with two round pointed prongs is excellent for removing roots of weeds such as couch grass penetrating the root systems of garden plants, and a little spatula-like double-ended steel 'widger' is helpful in weeding the rock garden.

Cultivators, consisting of curved, spear-bladed or plain prongs, on short and long handles are helpful in breaking up and aerating the soil, but need careful use among crops if many roots are not to be broken. They can be very tiring to use.

A **garden line** will be much needed in the vegetable garden for row-crop sowing and planting, and can be home-made with two hardwood or steel pegs and a bricklayer's chalk line, if funds do not run to the Skirret pattern of a steel pin and a line on a revolving reel.

A **wheelbarrow** repays its cost where there is much carting to be done, of soil, plant wastes, lawn mowings, fallen leaves and the like. They range from small capacity kinds with galvanised steel bodies, to large wooden or all-steel types with pneumatic rubber wheels (useful for use over turf) and the glass-fibre bodied, plastic ball-wheeled (functional but ugly), or two-wheeled trucks.

Trimming Tools Good secateurs live in a gardener's pocket for the clean surgical removal of broken, diseased and dying plant shoots, the checking of exuberant growth, and the regulatory pruning of shrubs, trees, and fruit bearing plants. The most efficient are those with the cutting blade closing on to an anvil (eg Rolcut), or slicing against a thicker stationary bottom blade (eg Felco, Wilkinson Sword), as they are less likely to twist and 'spring' than those with a scissors cutting action. Long-arm shoot pruners, heavy branch pruners and saws may be needed to tackle a jungle, or older established shrubs and trees, on occasion. But the best tool for the regular pruning of roses, shrubs and soft-wood plants, and for taking cuttings for propagation is the razor-sharp pruning knife, used cleanly and precisely to make the smoothest cuts.

With hedges in the garden, **hedging shears** are necessary. Look for good balance, blades heavy enough not to twist on tough shoots, and cutting edges easily kept sharp with a carborundum slip-stone, and heavy enough to permit re-hollow-grinding. Straight-edged blades are easier to care for than serrated. A Teflon coating eases cutting but wears in time. With lengthy lawn edges to trim, you may need a long-handled **grass shear.**

A small hand sickle, preferably with a curved solid blade, is very handy for trimming hedge bottoms, and odd corners, and where there is long grass to tackle periodically, the 'Turk' pattern of scythe is easier to master and use than the longer-bladed heavy kind.

Tools for Watering Watering cans should be light, easy to carry, balanced for easy use, with good reaching spouts and non-drip roses—very difficult to obtain. For garden use plastic types of 7–9 l/1½–2 gal capacity are excellent, especially those moulded in one piece. Their colour is an added attraction, and a good polythene plastic is likely to outlive metal. A second can which can be fitted with a sprinkler boom is worth buying for exclusive use with weed-killing solutions. A smaller watering can with a long tapering spout may be needed in looking after pot plants.

It is easier and more effective to water by hose-pipe and sprinkler or trickle piping than by watering can, and in laying out a new garden, it is well worth while putting in underground piping in alkathene plastic, 15–20cm/6–8in deep, to strategic points where a hose can be connected. This gets rid of trucking out hose reels and stands, and modern systems with easy-fit connections and fittings make the investment worth while. While rubber hose is excellent, the much cheaper and lighter hoses in PVC plastic are as serviceable and durable.

Power Tools undoubtedly help you to get through garden work in less time and with less effort. Straightforward spadework turns over $16–21m^2/18–23yd^2$ per hour. A power-driven cultivator should quarter the time. It also needs more space for manoeuvring, wider spaced row crops, costs more in capital and running, and will spend many days idle. It is usually cheaper to hire a power tool for specific jobs needing only a limited time to carry out. Power tools are not always labour-saving as concentration and pace take their toll.

There is a wide choice of power cultivators from small lightweight machines for the small garden to miniature tractors for the estate. They are powered by petrol/oil engines, 2-stroke or 4-stroke, the latter usually the more powerful and reliable, and there is at least one electrically driven. Most of them have ancillary tools for attachment, to tackle other jobs than just soil-turning, but the ease with which this can be done and the robustness of the equipment should be checked.

Cultivators work by ploughing—slicing and inverting a ribbon of soil, or by rotary action—milling the soil with a wheel of cutting blades or spring-loaded steel teeth. Ploughed soil needs further working, discing or cultivating, or harrowing to break it up. Rotary cultivation leaves the soil more or less pulverised and more prepared for sowing or planting, and can incorporate top-dressings efficiently. These machines do not cultivate as deeply and as thoroughly as the spade and fork, since they are designed to operate at not more than 16cm/6in deep. There is a tendency, with repeated use, for a somewhat impervious pan to form, which then has to be broken up.

Power can save time and energy in the repetitive chore of lawn mowing. There is a choice of machines in various sizes, with cylinder or rotating cutters, and driven by a 2-stroke or 4-stroke petrol/oil engine, or by electric motor, which may be battery driven, or mains-driven by means of a cable plugged into a power-circuit point. Electric drive means a much quieter machine, easier to stop and re-start. The small electric mowers for small lawns are excellent, once the management of the cable has been mastered. With a battery, a mower is free of tether, but the battery needs regular re-charging, and proper winter care when not being used.

Petrol-driven mowers need annual overhauling. The hover type of rotary mower has had a great vogue, works splendidly on the flat and on gentle slopes, but it develops a spongy, springy sward with the constant return of clippings to the surface. It needs care and not a little strength to keep it flat on rough ground and where cutting longish grass, and should be used strictly as advised by the makers.

Another area where the power tool can save much time is in hedge cutting and trimming. Again, it is often more economical to hire a power hedge-trimmer when needed, and where hedges are not extensive. The electrically-driven tool, off battery or mains, is the more common, and for ownership should be chosen for its cleanness of cut and of a size ample to do the work contemplated.

Power tools do need to be properly oiled and maintained, and periodically serviced and overhauled, and a careful reading of the maker's instruction and recommendations is as important as reading sowing or planting directions for plants.

6
Hedging for Shelter and Ornament

Well chosen hedging provides the most appropriate permanent living framework in the garden, cheaper than solid walling or fencing, and better able to absorb noise, tame wind and weather, with privacy, shelter and ornamental values. Plants for hedging are, however, drawn from upright-growing trees and shrubs which stand up well to restriction, and can resume their natural bent to make large, overwhelming growth in neglect.

Consider purpose first: boundary hedging for privacy and impenetrability to intruders—background hedging to shrub or flower border—hedging to break up wind and weather and give shelter—hedging to line paths, frame features or provide interior ornamentation—hedging for internal divisions and as features in themselves?

Second, bear in mind that your choice must be of plants suited to the environmental and growing conditions of the garden, of soil, exposure, and climate.

Rate of growth needs careful consideration. Broadly, low first cost and quick growth mean frequent trimming and high maintenance with short life. The slower-growing hedges are the more long-lived, and easier and less costly to keep trim and at required heights. Evergreens give all-the-year-round privacy and colour; deciduous hedging, with the exception of beech and hornbeam, grows quickly but is bare in winter.

For Boundaries and Backgrounds The cheapest hardy and adaptable evergreen for hedging is privet (*Ligustrum ovalifolium*), growing quickly and handsomely almost anywhere, but needs frequent trimming, and has greedy roots. For long-lived hedges that look better year by year a choice of holly (*Ilex aquifolium*), box (*Boxus sempervirens*) or yew (*Taxus baccata*) is hard to better; all being very hardy, adaptable to most soils and situations including shade, though the yew should not be used where grazing animals can reach. They need trimming only once a year in August to keep them groomed.

The winter-flowering laurustinus (*Viburnum tinus*) and the fragrant spring-flowering *Osmarea* × *burkwoodii* make unusual hedges up to 180cm/72in, with patience, and *Euonymus japonicus* is equally hardy for a seacoast or town garden. The small-leafed semi-evergreen Chinese bush honeysuckles (*Lonicera nitida* and stiffer var *L. fertilis*) grow rapidly, need clipping often, but make cheaply established hedges of up to 150cm/60in in any soil, and can be grown from cuttings. More pleasing, however, are hedges of some of the Escallonias such as *E. ingramii*, *E.* × 'Red Hedger', for up to 150–180cm/60–72in.

The firethorns make strong hedges under restriction, the hybrid *Puracantha* × 'Orange Glow' being most attractive for its glossy green evergreen foliage, flowering in early summer, and orange-red winter berries.

Deciduous Hedges   To make good thickets, deciduous hedges must be kept well trimmed. The cheapest is the native hawthorn or quick, *Crataegus monogyna*, planted in double rows, on most soils. Several flowering plums make tall decorative hedges but need good and not too acid soil— *Prunus cerasifera* 'Greenglow', *P. c. atropurpurea* 'Purple Flash', with green and copper-purple foliage respectively, with spring flowers, can be planted separately or mixed, for hedges from 120–200cm/48–80in. For a garden on the coast, an outer hedge of sea buckthorn, *Hippophae rhamnoides*, with its spiny shoots, narrow silvery leaves, orange berries, makes a salt-wind resistant windbreak, and intruder-proof tall hedge, under good trimming. The cotoneasters throw up erect-growing stems freely from the base to make sturdy hedges, usually semi-evergreen and berrying well, and *C. simonsii*, *C. lactea*, and *C. wardii* are good for this. The spring-flowering

56

Forsythia × intermedia spectabilis is ever eager to make new growth under frequent clipping, and goes on producing its golden-yellow flowers each April.

With beech, *Fagus sylvatica*, and its purple-leafed form, *purpurea*, you can make hedges and screens of any desirable height which will retain their brown leaves each winter, and for the heavy clay soils less suited to beech you can use horn-beam, *Carpinus betulus*, to similar purpose. On a really damp soil, the dawn redwood, *Metasequoia glyptostroboides*, is striking, with feathery green foliage that turns brown and gold in autumn before falling, and is one of the few deciduous conifers.

Flowering Hedges Many flowering shrubs can be planted hedge-like in rows, arcs or angle-wise within the garden, where they can be grown with informality and have room to spread their new growth each year after a post-blossom pruning. Good evergreens are *Berberis darwinii*, orange flowering, *B. × stenophylla*, yellow flowers, in April; the Mexican Orange, *Choisya ternata*, white fragrant flowers in early spring; and *Pyracantha coccinea lalandli* for its white June flowers, and autumn red berries; while fine deciduous kinds are the flowering currants, *Ribes sanguineum* and vars, for their scented red flower clusters in spring; *Spiraea × vanhouttei*, and *S. arguta*, billowing white each spring; the dwarf lilac, *Syringa palibiniana*, rose flowering in June; *Berberis thunbergii*, with spring yellow flowers, and its purple-leafed form *atropurpurea*. For mild localities, *Fuchsia magellanica* and vars *F. gracilis*, *F. versicolor*, 'Margaret', 'Mrs Popple', and *F. riccartonii* flower attractively with their ear-drop dangles through the summer.

Dwarf Hedges Invaluable for lining paths, marking garden divisions and fronting beds and borders, the low growing and dwarf hedging plants are beautiful and labour-saving. Among the best are *Euonymus radicans variegata* with silver-variegated foliage; and the grey-leafed *Senecio greyii*, rather sprawly to 100cm/40in, with yellow daisy flowers in summer; the sweetly scented lavenders, *Lavandula spica* to 100cm/40in, or its dwarfer forms 'Hidcote' and 'Munstead'; and *Santolina* *chamaecyparissus*, the silvery Lavender Cotton, and its more compact form *S. corsica*, with yellow button flowers in summer; New Zealand Veronicas such as *Hebe × andersonii*, 'Carl Teschner', and 'Blue Gem', for summer flowering; and the winter-flowering heaths in their compact forms such as *Erica carnea* 'Cecilia M. Beale', white; 'Ruby Glow', dark red; *E. vivellii*, carmine; and 'Winter Beauty', rose pink; and *E. mediterranea*, in forms 'Glauca', pale pink; and 'W. T. Racliff', white, compact and upright to 100cm/40in.

Planting   For a single line hedge, a trench about 60cm/24in wide should be dug, for a double line 90cm/36in, forking over the second spit well. A light soil needs fibrous organic matter; a heavy one gypsum and grit. A good sprinkling of bonemeal along with well broken rotted organic manure, peat or compost should be mixed with the top spit. Strong growing hedge plants may be set 30–60cm/12–24in apart; but for thick dense hedges of such plants as beech, hawthorn, hornbeam, or honeysuckle, double rows are planted, 30cm/12in apart, with plants 45cm/18in apart in staggered formation thus: ·.·.·.·.·.·.·.·. A hedge next to a wall or fence needs to be placed at least 45cm/18in from it.

Deciduous hedges are best planted in mild weather periods between October and March; while evergreen and coniferous hedges need to be planted either in October–November or late March–May, when conditions favour their ready recovery and renewed growth. At other times, plants can be set out of containers, provided care is taken to do this without the root ball losing soil. After planting, new hedges benefit from copious overhead watering in dry periods, especially in spring, with temporary shelter from drying winds, and they can be foliar fed in summer.

Trimming   Newly planted hedges need no trimming until making active growth, when side shoots may be lightly trimmed in August the first year, and in May–June and August the second year. Central leading shoots, chiefly on tree species, are left uncut until up to the height desired, when they can be cut back in February to a suitably placed side or lateral shoot or bud.

When established with a good framework of branches and shoots to the base, hedges need trimming according to the rate of growth and kind. Quick-growing hedges (privet, honeysuckle, thorn, etc) need trimming 3 to 5 times a year between May and September to keep them formally neat. Formal hedges of box, holly, yew, other evergreens, and also beech and hornbeam need a major trim each year in late July or August, and perhaps a lighter one to trim any shagginess in March. They should be cut to have straight sides and flat top, or with sides tapering to the top, which can be rounded or peaked; but avoid a wider top than base.

7

Planting for Permanence

Planting for permanence concerns the selection and placing of those perennial woody plants—trees, shrubs and climbers—with which we frame the garden and unite it with the house, and live with from year to year. Such plants need to be chosen not merely for their beauty but also for their adaptability to the environmental circumstances we can give them. Most of all we need to visualise their growth to maturity and how it will affect the garden and its changing appearances.

A practical approach is to assess each choice in terms of (1) Likely mature height and breadth; (2) Form—upright, spreading, rounded, weeping; (3) Habit—deciduous, evergreen; (4) Foliage—colouring and shape; (5) Flowers—colour, season; (6) Fruits—colour, kind, edibility; (7) hardiness; (8) special soil needs, if any; (9) Exposure tolerance—to light, shade, wind, and drought.

Trees are woody perennials with a single stem or trunk from the ground up. They enlarge a garden to the sky, can give shelter and shade, obscure ugly views, and if well chosen, delight at all seasons. Forest trees—beech, ash, elm, chestnut, oaks, poplar, sycamore, lime—need space and become overpowering in small gardens; better to choose their smaller decorative forms—the silver-variegated leafed Norway maple, *Acer platanoides* v *drummondii*, the red horse-chestnut, *Aesculus* × *carnea briotii*, the airy silver birch, *Betula pendula* or its v *fastigiata*, the double-flowering Gean, *Prunus avium* v *plena*, the elegant hybrid lime, *Tilia* × *euchlora*, the rowan, *Sorbus aucuparia*, for chalky soils and wind tolerance.

There are, however, many smaller ornamental trees, growing to 5–10m/15–35ft well suited to modern gardens and sound first choices are:

Spring-flowering—the May thorns, *Crataegus oxycantha* in vars white double flowering *plena*, and scarlet 'Paul's Scarlet'; Golden Rain, *Laburnum × vossii*; the almond, *Prunus dulcis* v *macrocarpa*, March bloom; the apricot, *Prunus mume* v 'beni-shi-don'; the peaches, *Prunus persica* v 'Helen Borchers', 'Iceberg' or 'Klara Mayer'; the Japanese flowering cherries, *Prunus serrulata* in vars 'Ojochin', 'Shimidsu Sakura', 'Shirofugen', 'Sargentii', 'Tai Haku', 'Sekiyama' ('Kanzan'); the more delicate Spring Cherry, *Prunus subhirtella* and its vars *flore pleno*, and *stellata*; the crab apples, *Malus floribunda*, M. × 'Profusion', M. × 'Simcoe', and *Magnolia kobus* for all but chalky soils.

Summer-flowering trees are few, but *Koelreuteria paniculata* is highly attractive in colourful foliage, and has panicles of yellow flowers, and *Eucryphia glutinosa* is worth trying, trained as a tree, for its abundant white summer flowers.

Autumn foliage colour—the Maple, *Acer palmatum* 'Heptolobum Osakazuki'; for scarlet hues; the orange-red Thorn, *Cratageus prunifolia*, also with showy haws; the crimson-gold Ironwood, *Parrotia persica*; the Mountain Ash, *Sorbus ×* 'Joseph Rock', with amber-yellow autumn tints; and Silver Birches, *Betula ermanii* and *B. jacquemontii*, colour golden.

Winter Fruits and Berries—*Cotoneaster ×* 'Cornubia', red berried clusters; *C. × watereri* and forms, red and orange red berries, tree-like with training are magnificent; *Malus* 'Golden Hornet', 'John Downie', and *M. hupehensis* are the pick of crab apples with colourful fruits; and the pinnate-leafed *Sorbus scalaris, S. ×* 'Winter Cheer', keep their clusters of red, and orange-red berries well into winter.

Narrowly erect, fastigiate Japanese flowering Cherry, *Prunus serrulata* v *erecta* or 'Amanogawa' is unique in habit, and a column of soft pink bloom in April–May, for confined spaces, specimen or group planting. For a green summer pyramid of foliage, the hornbeam, *Carpinus betulus fastigiata*, becomes a column of rich brown withered leaves for winter.

Trees with weeping habit make good lawn or courtyard specimens, especially the weeping birch, *Betula pendula* v *youngii*, the weeping spring cherry, *Prunus subhirtella* v *pendula* or *pendula rosea*, and the weeping willow-leafed pear, *Pyrus salicifolia* v *pendula*—all safer choices than the golden weeping willow, *Salix* × *chrysocoma*, for soils which are naturally moist or near water.

Evergreen Trees   So far, we have considered deciduous trees, and evergreen trees are less numerous. The strawberry tree, *Arbutus unedo* or its hybrid *A.* × *andrachnoides*, are handsome and lime-tolerant, but take some years to produce their waxen-white, urn-shaped flowers, and round strawberry coloured and pimpled fruits. The holly, *Ilex aquifolium*, grows tree-like, given free rein, and good forms are the silver holly, *I. argenteomarginata*, the yellow variegated 'Golden King', the bright green, free-berrying *I. pyramidalis*, and 'Madame Briot' with dark yellow-margined leaves, but being unisexual, these females need a male accompanying them such as 'Golden Queen' or 'Silver Queen', which are males despite incongruous naming.

Conifers   For other evergreens, go to the conifers. Excluding the tall, large species best suited to forests, arboretums or parklands, such as cedars, firs, pines, spruces or redwoods, a nucleus can be chosen for specimen, group, or avenue planting, or in the case of the dwarf kinds for association with low-growing ericas and ground cover plants, and as accent plants in the rock garden or border. Conifers do like clean unpolluted air, open situations, deepish soils, and freedom from blasting dry winds and draughts. Be dubious of the word 'dwarf', for many conifers, although slow-growing, become quite tall in time.

Planting Trees   Deciduous trees are planted while leafless, from October to March, given mild weather and easily worked soil; while evergreens and conifers may be planted in late September to November or March to May. In each case, a planting site somewhat larger than is needed to take the roots is prepared; taking out the topsoil to mix with one-third to one-half its bulk of compost, moist peat, leaf-mould or ground composted bark, and a sprinkling of John Innes

Base fertilizer. After breaking up the exposed subsoil, adding if necessary a soil conditioner, and refirming, the tree can be placed in position with roots evenly spread. Insert a stake if this is needed; and then fill in with the enriched topsoil, working and firming it to the roots, until covered, and water.

Evergreens and conifers are best planted out of pots or containers, or with their roots in a soil ball, and disturbed as little as possible. Newly planted trees need nursing through dry periods with overhead spraying and judicious watering, and sheltered from drying winds.

Shrubs and Their Choice Apart from being smaller, shrubs differ from trees in that they form several persistent woody stems from their base. Being easily maintained, they are labour-saving, and used imaginatively can provide colour and interest at all seasons. At the outset, it is best to concentrate on shrubs of suitable size, of a habit that does not need much pruning, and of a hardiness that ensures reliable flowering performance, and good looks when out of flower.

Tall, shapely shrubs can be used for specimen planting. Those of symmetrical outline enhance formal lines, but shrubs lend themselves best to informal planning, to adorn corners, wide single or double borders, or island beds, with the taller, merging to medium-sized in the middle, and dwarf types at the edges, but not necessarily uniformly, however. Whether planted singly or in groups, each plant should have sufficient room to grow and display its qualities, spaced at about half their mature spread at planting. Judicious placing of everygreens also offsets winter bareness of deciduous shrubs.

Carpeting Shrubs Several dwarf and prostrate growing shrubs are excellent as a means of reducing the need for weed control. The best are the evergreens with close dense foliage such as the heaths (Erica spp), *Euonymus radicans fortunei* v *radicans* and its v *variegatus*, *Hebe* × 'Autumn Glory', *Hebe* × *pagei*, and Helianthemums in variety, for open sunny locations; while Ivies (*Hedera helix* vars), *Hypericum calycinum*, *Pachysandra terminalis*, *Rubus calycinoides*, and the Periwinkles, *Vinca major* and *V. minor* with their varieties, excel in light shade and under trees.

A Pick of Ornamental and Flowering Shrubs

Name of shrub	Deciduous/ Evergreen	Height approx	Flowers	Berries	Autumn colour	Position
Spring-flowering						
Berberis aggregata hybrids	D	1.5m	yellow	coral-red	good	sun–light shade
Berberis darwinii	E	2m	orange	fair		sun–partial shade
Berberis × *stenophylla* v *coccinea*, etc	E	3m	yellow	fair		sun–partial shade
Camellia japonica in variety	E	2m up	red, pink white			sheltered light shade acid soil
Chaenomeles japonica (Maules Quince)	D	1m	orange-red	fair		sun–partial shade
Cytisus × *beanii*	semi-E	35cm	yellow	pods		sun
Cytisus × *praecox*	D	40cm	cream	pods		sun
Cytisus scoparius in named varieties	D	2m	various	pods		sun
Erica mediterranea and varieties	E	.5–1m	rose, pink, white			open sun; lime tolerant
Forsythia × *intermedia* vs *spectabilis* 'Lynwood'	D	2m	yellow			sun–partial shade
Kerria japonica and v *pleniflora*	D	to 2m	rich yellow		green stems	sun–partial shade
Magnolia stellata	D	2–3m	white*			sun–light shade
Osmarea × *burkwoodii*	E	2–3m	white*			sun–partial shade
Prunus × *cistena*	D	2m	white*	purple	rich red	sun–light shade
Ribes sanguineum in vs 'Pulborough Scarlet', *splendens*	D	1.5m	crimson*	blue-black	fair	sun–partial shade
Skimmia japonica vs	E	1m	white*	red		shade tolerant
Spiraea × *arguta*	D	1.5m	white			sun–partial shade
Syringa (Lilac) vs and hybrids	D	to 3m	white* purple*			sun
Viburnum × *burkwoodii*	E	2.5m	white*			sun–partial shade
Viburnum × *juddii*	D	2m	white*			sun–light shade
Viburnum opulus sterile	D	1.5m	white		fair	sun–partial shade
Weigela florida v *variegata*	D	1.5m	pink		cream and pink	sun–light shade
For Lime-free, humus-rich soils						
Azalea, Ghent hybrids	D	to 2m	various*		rich	open sun–light shade
Azalea, Knap Hill hybrids	D	1.8–2m	various			
Azalea, Mollis hybrids	D	to 1.8m	various		rich	light shade, shelter
Azalea, Japanese hybrids eg Kurume, Vuyk	E	.5–1.2m	various			light shade, shelter
Enkianthus campanulatus	D	2–5m	sulphur		yellow/ red	open–light shade
Pieris floribunda	E	1.5m	white			partial shade
Pieris formosa v *forrestii*	E	2.5m	white		exceptional (in spring)	partial shade
Rhododendron spp and hybrids	E	2–5m	various			light or partial shade
Rhododendron, dwarf hybrids	E	.5–1.5m	various			light or partial shade

* good for fragrance

Name of shrub	Deciduous/ Evergreen	Height approx	Flowers	Berries	Autumn colour	Position
Summer-flowering						
Buddleia alternifolia	D	to 10m	lilac*			sun
Ceanothus × 'Gloire de Versailles'	D	2m	deep blue			sun–light shade
Ceanothus × *veitchianus*	E	2m	blue			sun–light shade
Cistus × 'Silver Pink'	E	.6m	pink			sun–shelter
Deutzia scabra vars	D	3m	white			sun–light shade

Name of shrub	Deciduous/ Evergreen	Height approx	Flowers	Berries	Autumn colour	Position
Escallonia × hybrids, 'Donard' vars	E	1.5–3m	rose, pink, white			sun–partial shade
Genista tinctoria v 'Royal Gold'	D	1m	yellow			sun
Hebe × 'Card Teschner'	E	.5m	violet			sun–light shade
Helianthemum num mularium 'Ben' vars	D	25cm	various			full sun–dry soils
Hydrangea macrophylla Hortensia vars.	D	1.5–2m	white, red, pink, blue			sun–light shade
Hypericum forrestii	semi-E	1m	golden		rich	sun–shade
Hypericum × 'Hidcote'	semi-E	1.7m	golden		tinted	sun–shade
Lavendula spica and vs	E	.6–1m	blue*			sun–light shade
Magnolia grandiflora v 'Goliath'	E	2.5m	creamy white			warm sun– shelter
Olearia × *haastii*	E	1.5m	white*			sun–partial shade
Philadelphus × 'Belle Etoile' and hybrids	D	2m	white*			sun–light shade
Potentilla fruticosa in variety	D	to 1m	yellows, white			sun–shade
Rosa, shrub species	D	1–2m	various*			sun–light shade
Santolina chamaecyparissus	E	.3m	yellow		silver	sun
Senecio greyii	E	to 1m	yellow		grey	sun
Sorbaria aitchisonii	D	2m	white			sun–light shade
Spiraea × 'Anthony Waterer'	D	1m	crimson			sun
Tamarix pentandra	D	to 2m	rose-pink		brown	sun–near the coast

For lime-free, humus-rich soils

Name of shrub	Deciduous/ Evergreen	Height approx	Flowers	Berries	Autumn colour	Position
Daboecia cantabrica vs	E	.6m	purple			sun
Erica cinerea in var (Bell Heather)	E	25cm	various			sun
Erica vagans in var (Cornish Heath)	E	.6m	white, pinks			sun
Calluna vulgaris in var (Heather)	E	.15–.5m	pink, red, white			open sun

* good for fragrance

Autumn Flowering

Name of shrub	Deciduous/ Evergreen	Height approx	Flowers	Berries	Autumn colour	Position
Buddleia davidii in variety	D	to 3m	blues, mauve*, white, purple			sun–light shade
B. d. nanhoensis vs	D	1.2m	purple, white			sun–light shade
Ceratostigma willmottianum	D	to 1m	rich blue		red tinted	sun–light shade
Caryopteris × *clandonensis*	D	.6m	blue			sun–warm shelter
Fatsia japonica	E	2m	white			shade
Fuchsia magellanica v *riccartonii*	D	1m	red and purple			sun–light shade
Hebe × 'Autumn Glory'	E	to 1m	violet			sun–light shade
Hibiscus syriacus in variety	D	to 2m	yellows, pinks, red			hot sun
Hydrangea × *preziosa*	D	1.5m	rose-pink		purple	sun–light shade
Hydrangea villosa	D	1.5m	lilac			sun–light shade
Potentilla arbuscula, vs	D	.5m	yellow			sun–light shade
Rhus (*Cotinus*) *coggygria* and vs	D	to 3m	fawn		rich purples	open sun
Romneya coulteri and vs	D	to 1m	white			sun–warm shelter

Name of shrub	Deciduous/ Evergreen	Height approx	Flowers	Berries	Autumn colour	Position
Winter Flowering						
Corylopsis spicata	D	to 2m	primrose		fair	sun–shelter
Daphne laureola	E	to .6m	yellow-green			shade
Daphne mezereum and vs	D	to 1m	mauve, white, red			shade
Erica carnea and vs	E	to .2m	pinks, red, white			open, sun
Erica × darleyensis vs	E	to .6m	pinks, white			open, sun
Hamamelis × 'Jelena'	D	to 2m	yellow-red		very rich	sun–light shade
Hamamelis mollis and v pallida	D	to 2m	golden*, sulphur*		yellow	sun–light shade
Garrya elliptica (male)	E	2m	grey-green			sun-light shade
Mahonia japonica	E	2m	yellow*			light shade
Mahonia × media 'Charity'	E	2m	yellow*			light shade
Lonicera × purpusii	D	1.5m	cream*			sun
Viburnum × bodnantense vs 'Dawn', 'Deben'	D	2.5m	rose-pink*		fair	warm sun
Viburnum tinus, vars	E	2m	white			open sun–shade

* good for fragrance

The Pruning of Shrubs and Trees

The Pruning of Shrubs and Trees When well chosen and sited to exhibit the most of their natural form and habit, shrubs and trees should need little pruning, apart from the cutting out of dead or ailing wood as soon as seen. Otherwise, the rules are simple: (1) plants that flower in the first half of the year, up to the summer solstice (June 21), are best pruned as soon as flowers fade; (2) plants that flower in the second half of the year are best pruned when growth is at its nadir—usually February or early March.

A Pick of Hardy Climbing Shrubs and Wall Plants

Name of plant	Method of climbing	Deciduous Evergreen	Height	Flowering	Suitable aspects	Remarks
The True Climbers						
Akebia quinata	Twining	semi-E	10m	May	S. W. E.	looks good in trees
Campsis grandiflora	Self-clinging	D	6m	Aug–Sep	S. W.	needs warm sun
Clematis armandii vs	Tendrils	E	to 6m	Apl–May	S. W.	needs warm sun
Clematis × jackmanii	Tendrils	D	to 4m	Jul–Sep	any	reliable
Clematis montana vs	Tendrils	D	to 9m	May	any	very vigorous
Clematis × hybrids	Tendrils	D	to 6m	June–Sep	any	need 2–3 yrs before flowering
Hedera helix vs (Ivy)	Self-clinging	E	to 9m	Aug	any	chiefly foliage
Hydrangea petiolaris	Self-clinging	D	to 20m	June	W. N. E.	autumn leaf/tint
Jasminum officinale	Twining	D	to 9m	Jun–Sep	S. W.	likes sun
Lonicera × americana	Twining	D	to 9m	Jun–Jul	S. W.	scented flowers
Lonicera japonica v aureoreticulata	Twining / Twining	E / semi-E	to 10m / to 6m	Jun–Aug / ?	any / S. W. E.	scented flowers / for foliage beauty
Lonicera periclymenum v *serotina*	Twining	D	to 6m	Jul–Oct	W. N. E.	scented flowers
Parthenocissus henryana	Self-clinging	D	to 10m	tiny	S. W.	for foliage beauty

Name of plant	Method of climbing	Deciduous Evergreen	Height	Flowering	Suitable aspects	Remarks
Parthenocissus × veitchii	Self-clinging	D	to 9m	—	any	for foliage beauty
Passiflora caerulea	Twining tendril	D	to 5m	Jul–Sep	S. W.	needs warm sun
Pileostegia viburnoides	Self-clinging	E	to 6m	Aug–Oct	S. W. N.	slow-growing
Polygonum bladschunicum	Twining	D	to 12m	Jul–Sep	any	rampant growth
Vitis × 'Brant'	Tendrils	D	to 8m	May	S. W.	hardy grape vine
Vitis coignetiae	Tendrils	D	to 15m	May	S. W.	v. large leaves
Wisteria × macrobotrys	Twining	D	to 6m	May–Jun	S. W.	for arbours, etc
Wisteria sinensis, vs	Twining	D	to 20m	May	S. W.	for large areas

Tall-growing 'Wall' Shrubs

Name of plant	Method of climbing	Deciduous Evergreen	Height	Flowering	Suitable aspects	Remarks
Ceanothus × 'Delight'		E	to 5m	May	S. W.	for sun and shelter
Ceanothus × 'Autumnal Blue'		E	to 5m	Aug–Oct	S. W.	prune in April
Choisya ternata		E	1.2m	May	S. W.	good for corners
Cotoneaster horizontalis		D	1.2m	May	N. E. W.	autumn berries
Cotoneaster microphyllus		E	.5m	May	any	autumn berries
Chanaemoles speciosa vs		D	2m	Mar	any	flowering japonica
Forsythia suspensa vs		D	3m	Mar–Apl	any	v *sieboldii* for N
Jasminum nudiflorum		D	to 3m	Nov–Feb	any	indispensable
Osmanthus delavayi		D	to 2m	Apl	S. W.	scented flowers
Prunus triloba		D	to 2m	Mar–Apl	S. W.	prune in May
Pyracantha atalantioides		E	to 4m	May	any	autumn berries
Pyracantha coccinea and v		E	to 4m	May	any	autumn berries
Pyracantha rogersiana and v		E	to 4m	May	any	autumn berries
Rosa (Roses) rambler		D	to 3m	Jun–July	S. W. E.	'Mermaid' for N.
Rosa ever-blooming climbers		D	to 2m	Jun–Oct	S. W.	Danse du Feu, etc
Rosa climbing sports HT		D	to 3m	Jun–Sep	S. W. E.	prune in winter
Viburnum plicatum v *tomentosum*		D	to 3m	May–Jun	S. W. E.	autumn leaf tints

Perennial Planting Flowering herbaceous perennial plants show their paces in the season following planting. They can be used to furnish borders in their own right, as corner or island beds, or interplanted with shrubs.

Such plants are more vulnerable to hard winter weather than woody perennials, and are best planted in September–October or March–April. The soil in which they are planted should be mixed with moist peat or ground bark or rotted organic matter and a mixture of equal parts by weight of hoof and horn meal (or slow release nitrogen) and bonemeal, at 60–80g per m^2/ 2–3oz per yd^2, well firmed to the roots, and dressed with a slug and snail deterrent (metaldehyde, methiocarb).

About 4–6 plants per m^2/yd^2 will be needed. Groups of three or more are more effective than single plants.

A Pick of Hardy Herbaceous Perennial Flowering Plants

Name of plant	Height approx	Flowering period	Aspect	Soil preferences
Spring Flowering				
Ajuga pyramidalis	20cm	May–June	sun/shade	moist
Bergenia cordifolia etc	25cm	May	shade	ordinary
Brunnera macrophylla	30cm	Apl–June	part shade	moist average
Dicentra eximea, D. spectabilis	45cm	May–July	part shade	average, moist
Doronicum 'Miss Mason', etc	45cm	Apl–May	part shade	moist
Euphorbia wulfenii	1m	Apl–July	sun	ordinary
Geum × 'Fire Opal'; 'Georgenburg'	60cm	May–July	sun	ordinary
Helleborus orientalis vs	60cm	Apl–May	part shade	humus-rich
Hosta crispula, H. fortunei	60cm	May–June	part shade	average
Iris × Bearded hybrids	to 1m	May–June	sun	average
Nepeta × *faassenii*	45cm	June–Aug	sun	humus-rich ordinary
Polemonium foliossisimum and vs	75cm	May–Aug	sun	ordinary
Trollius europaeus and vs	75cm	May–June	sun/shade	ordinary but moist
Summer Flowering				
Achillea clypeolata	45cm	June–Aug	sun	well-drained
Achillea filipendula vs	to 1m	June–Aug	sun	well-drained
Aconitum napellus vs	1–1.5m	July–Aug	sun	ordinary
Anaphalis margaritacea and sp	45cm	July–Sep	sun	ordinary
Anchusa azurea and vs	1–1½m	June–July	sun	ordinary
Aquilegia × hybrids	to .8m	June–July	sun	ordinary
Aruncus sylvester and v	1.5m	June–July	sun/shade	ordinary but not dry
Aster alpinus, A. yunnanensis	20–30cm	June–July	sun	ordinary
Astible × *arendsii* and vs	60–65cm	July–Aug	sun/shade	humus-rich, moist
Campanula glomerata and vs	30–60cm	June–Aug	sun	ordinary
Campanula lactiflora and vs	to 1.4m	June–Sep	sun	ordinary
Campanula persicifolia and vs	30–90cm	July–Aug	sun/shade	ordinary
Centaurea dealbata and vs	60cm	July–Sep	sun	ordinary
Coreopsis grandiflora and vs	60–90cm	June–Aug	sun	ordinary
Chrysanthemum maximum and vs	60–90cm	July–Aug	sun	ordinary
Delphinium × hybrids	to 1.6m	June–July	sun	deep, well-drained
Echinops ritro v 'Blue Cloud'	to 1.2m	July–Aug	sun	ordinary
Erigeron × hybrids	45–60cm	June–Aug	sun	well-drained
Eryngium alpinum and vs	to 75cm	June–Aug	sun	dry, well-drained
Gaillardia aristata and vs	60–90cm	July–Sep	sun	ordinary
Gypsophila paniculata and vs	60–90cm	June–Aug	sun	ordinary, likes lime
Helenium autumnale and vs	1–1.5m	July–Sep	sun	ordinary
Heliopsis scabra and vs	1–1.5m	June–Sep	sun	ordinary
Hemerocallis × hybrids	to 1.2m	June–Aug	sun	ordinary
Heuchera sanguinea and vs	45–60cm	June–July	sun	ordinary
Hosta plantaginea, H. undulata, vs	45cm	July–Sep	sun/shade	humus-rich
Iris kaempferi and vs	60–90cm	June–Aug	sun/p. shade	moist, lime-free
Kniphofia galpinii, K. uveria, vs	30–90cm	June–Sep	sun	ordinary
Liatris callilepis	to 1m	Aug–Sep	sun	well-drained light
Lupinus polyphyllus hybrids	to 1.5m	June–Aug	sun	ordinary
Lychnis chalcedonica, L. flos-jovis	60–90cm	July–Aug	sun	well-drained
Lythrum salicaria and vs	75–90cm	July–Sep	sun	moist

A spring bedding scheme. Tulips mix very well with wallflowers

A formal edging to a bed accentuating the colour behind. There are plenty of grey and silver leaved plants suitable for every kind of soil

Name of plant	Height approx	Flowering period	Aspect	Soil preferences
Monarda didyma and vs	to 1m	July–Aug	sun/shade	moist
Paeonia lactiflora vs	to 1m	June–July	sun/shade	humus-rich soil
Phlox maculata and vs	70–90cm	July–Sep	sun	good, ordinary
Potentilla atrosanguinea vs	30–45cm	June–Aug	sun	dryish
Rudbeckia fulgida, R. laciniata vs	7–2m	July–Oct	sun	deep, heavyish
Salvia × superba, named vs	to 1m	July–Sep	sun/shade	ordinary
Scabiosa caucasia vs	45–60cm	July–Sep	sun	well-drained, likes lime
Stachys lanata, S. spicata vs	30–45cm	June–Aug	sun/shade	well-drained
Thalictrum dipterocarpum and vs	to 1.5m	July–Aug	sun	well-drained, moist
Tradescantia viginiana vs	45–60cm	June–Sep	sun	ordinary
Verbascum hybridum vs	$1–1\frac{1}{2}$m	July–Aug	sun	well-drained, likes chalk
Veronica spicata and vs	30–60cm	July–Aug	sun	ordinary
Veronica teucrium vs	30–60cm	July–Aug	sun	ordinary

A Pick of Hardy Herbaceous Flowering Plants

Name of plant	Height approx	Flowering period	Aspect	Soil preferences
Anaphalis yedoensis	to 90cm	Aug–Oct	sun/dry shade	well-drained
Anemone elegans and vs	to 1m	Aug–Oct	sun/shade	ordinary
Anemone hupehensis and vs	to 1m	Aug–Oct	sun/shade	ordinary
Aster amellus and vs	60cm	Aug–Sep	sun	ordinary
Aster linosyris vs	60cm	Aug–Oct	sun	ordinary
Aster novae-angliae hybrids	to $1\frac{1}{2}$m	Aug–Oct	sun/shade	ordinary
Aster novae-belgii hybrids	to 1m	Aug–Oct	sun	ordinary
Coreopsis rosea	30cm	Sep–Oct	sun	ordinary
Hyssopus aristatus	30cm	Sep–Oct	sun	dryish
Sedum spectabiles and vs	30–45cm	Aug–Oct	sun	ordinary
Serratula shawii	20cm	Sep–Oct	sun	ordinary
Solidago canadensis and vs	1–2m	Aug–Sep	sun	ordinary
Sidalcea × hybrid vs	1m	Aug–Sep	sun	ordinary

Winter Flowering

Name of plant	Height approx	Flowering period	Aspect	Soil preferences
Helleborus atrorubens	30cm	Nov–Feb	part shade	humus-rich
Helleborus corsicus	60cm	Feb–Apl	part shade	humus-rich
Helleborus niger	30cm	Jan–Feb	part shade	humus-rich
Iris foetidissima	to 60cm	Nov–Jan	sun/shade	for foliage effect
Iris unguicularis (stylosa)	18cm	Jan–Mar	sun/S. wall	well drained

8

For Instant Flowering

CULTURAL NEEDS OF BULBS AND CORMS

Most hardy bulbs and corms of flowering size do well in their first year wherever planted but to succeed perennially need soils of good drainage, laced with rotted, not fresh, organic compost or materials, and bonemeal, and feeding with a balanced fertilizer after flowering; in positions which are reasonably well sunned when they are in leaf.

They are planted while fully dormant, and can be placed at a depth of three times their height from base to shoulder or crown, and about three times their diameter apart. They can be left in situ, naturalized, for several years until overcrowded and producing fewer flowers; when they can be lifted, graded

A Pick of Flowering Bulbous Plants

Name of plant	When to plant	Soil	Situation	Depth to plant	Distance apart	Flowering time
Allium azureum, A. moly etc	Sep–Oct	any	sun	6–7cm	5–8cm	early summer
Camassia esculenta	Oct–Feb	moist	part shade	10cm	15cm	July
Chionodoxa luciliae, etc	Sep–Oct	well-drained	sun	7.5cm	5cm	March
Erythronium dens-canis	Sep–Nov	porous	sun	7.5cm	10cm	Apl–May
Fritillaria meleagris	Aug–Nov	porous	sun/shade	10cm	15cm	Apl–May
Galanthus nivalis, elwesii	Sep–Nov	any	sun/shade	2.5cm	2.5cm	Feb–Mar
Galtonia candicans	Sep–Oct	rich loam	part shade	15cm	30cm	July–Aug
Hyacinthus orientalis vs	Sep–Oct	rich loam	sun	12cm	15cm	Apl–May
Iris reticulata vs	Sep–Oct	porous	sun	5–6cm	10cm	Jan–Feb
Iris xiphiodes (English)	Sep–Nov	porous	sun	8cm	15cm	June–July
Iris xiphium (Spanish)	Sep–Oct	porous	sun	8cm	15cm	June
Iris hybrids (Dutch)	Sep–Oct	porous	sun	8–10cm	18cm	June
Lilium spp (Asiatic)	Oct–Mar	rich loam	part shade	15–20cm	16cm	June–Sep
Muscari armeniacum, etc	Sep–Oct	any	sun/shade	8cm	8cm	April
Narcissus spp and vs	Aug–Oct	any	sun	10–15cm	8–12cm	Mar–Apl
Puschkinia scilloides	Sep–Dec	porous	part shade	6cm	8cm	May
Scillabbifolia, siberica	Sep–Nov	porous	part shade	6cm	8cm	Mar–May
Tulipa: early flowering vs	Sep–Oct	loamy	sun	8–12cm	15–20cm	April
Tulipa: May flowering vs	Sep–Oct	loamy	sun	8–12cm	15–20cm	May
Tulipa spp	Sep–Oct	loamy	sun	8–10cm	10–15cm	Apl–May

A Pick of Flowering Cormous Plants

Name of plant	When to plant	Soil	Situation	Depth to plant	Distance apart	Flowering time
Colchicum autumnale vs	July–Aug	porous	sun	8cm	16cm	September
Crocus medius, speciosus	July	porous	sun	6cm	6–8cm	Sep–Nov
Crocus chrysanthus vs	Sep–Oct	porous	sun	8cm	6–8cm	Feb–Mar
Crocus tomasinianus vs	Sep–Oct	porous	sun	8cm	6–8cm	Feb–Mar
Crocus hybrids (Dutch)	Sep–Oct	porous	sun	8cm	8–10cm	April
Freesia × hybrids (prepared)	Apl–May	porous	sun	8cm	8cm	June–July
Gladiolus × hybrids*	March	porous	sun	12cm	16cm	July–Oct
*Gladiolus primulinus** vs	to May	porous	sun	12cm	16cm	July–Sep

* corms are lifted each November and stored cool

A Pick of Tuberous Flowering Plants

Name of plant	When to plant	Soil	Situation	Depth to plant	Distance apart	Flowering time
Anemone coronaria 'De Caen' 'St. Brigid' strains	Oct–Nov or	rich loam	warm sun	2.5cm	5–8cm	April
Anemone pavonina 'St Bavo'	Mar–Apl	rich loam	warm sun	2.5cm	5–8cm	Aug–Sep
Cyclamen europaeum and	June–	rich loam	part shade	1.5cm	8cm	Aug–Oct
Cyclamen neapolitanum	July	rich loam	part shade	1.5cm	8cm	Aug–Oct
Cyclamen orbiculatum vs	June–July	rich loam	part shade	1.5cm	8cm	Mar–Apl
Cyclamen repandum	June–July	rich loam	part shade	1.5cm	8cm	Mar–Apl
Begonia × hybrids, *B.* pendula vs	Mar–June	rich loam	part shade	1cm	8–10cm	summer
Dahlia × hybrids and vs	Apl–May	good loam	sun	3–6cm	15–20cm	summer
Eranthis hyemalis	Sep–Oct	porous	sun/shade	5–6cm	8cm	Feb–Mar

and replanted more thinly. Otherwise, it is sensible to remove spent flowerheads, feed, and leave plants to grow until leaves yellow and wither, when they may be lifted, and dried off in airy conditions, prior to storing cool until planting time comes round again. If plants must be lifted in green leaf, they should be dug up with roots in soil and replanted in a trench on spare ground to finish their growth cycle. The larger bulbs and corms are reserved for future flowering; smaller offsets planted in enriched soil to grow and build up to flowering sizes.

FLOWERS FROM ANNUALS

An annual is a plant which grows from seed, flowers and completes its life cycle within one season. In gardening, it may also be a plant which is perennial under warm native conditions but is grown for its first year performance here, and is winter-killed.

Annuals give gay colour quickly, often blooming for weeks, and can be used almost anywhere in the garden. They are usually divided into the half-hardy, derived from species native to warmer climes than our own, and which cannot be sown or grown out of doors until the danger of spring frosts is past—May–June; and hardy, which can be sown out of doors where they are to grow, usually in March–April.

Both half-hardy and annual seeds may be sown under heated conditions under glass, however, and subsequently planted or bedded out in order to have them in flower as early and for as long as possible. Some of the hardiest annuals (calendula, limnanthes, myosotis, papaver, and saponaria) may be sown outdoors in late summer, to overwinter and flower early in the following year.

Seeds and Their Germination   To germinate well, seeds need air, water, and warmth; not until root hairs form on the emerging root-radicle do they need nutrients. Air and moisture in the right balance, and a reserve of nutrients, particularly phosphates, are assured by the rooting medium—a prepared compost for use under glass, and/or prepared soil out of doors. But the critical factor in speed and vigour of germination is warmth; assured by a soil temperature (or bottom heat) of 21–24°C/70–76°F for half-hardy annuals, and of 18–21°C/ 65–70°F for hardy annuals.

The Use and Choice of Annuals   Ranging in size from 10cm– 2m/4–80in, annuals can be found to ornament most parts of the garden. A border of annuals can make a feature in itself. They may be used to edge paths or plantings of young perennials, even to fill in among them for their first year. They can help to furnish the new rock garden. The taller ones are good for temporary hedging, and climbers are good for trellis and walls or to nurse slower-growing specimens.

Biennial Bloom   Horticulturally, a biennial is a plant grown from seed one year, to flower the next. Some perennials are also grown as biennials in practice. The seeds are sown out of doors in late May to July, in seed-beds, thinly, and the seedlings either thinned or transplanted a few weeks later to 15–23cm/6–9in apart; and finally planted where they are to flower the following spring or summer, in September to early November; or if they are only wanted for summer-flowering may be transplanted in March.

A Pick of Annuals

Botanical name	Common name	Height in cm	Notable varieties	Colours
Hardy Annuals				
Alyssum maritimum	Madwort	8–10	Little Dorrit, Rosie O'Day, etc	white, rose pink
Calendula officinalis	Marigold	30–45	Juliette, Art Shades, Radio, etc	yellows, orange
Centaurea cyanus	Cornflower	30–90	Polka Dot, Julep, Mixed	blue, red, pink, white
Chrysanthemum carinatum	Chrysanthemum	50–60	Monarch Court Jesters, Mixed	yellow, purple, red
Clarkia elegans	Clarkia	60	Monarch Mixed, etc	pinks, purple, white
Convolvulus tricolor	Morning Glory	15–30	Blue Flash, Royal Ensign	Blue
Convolvulus major	Morning Glory	300	Mixed blue, white, etc	as a mixture
Dimorphotheca aurantiaca	Star of the Veldt	30	Las Vegas, hybrids	white to gold
Echium plantagineum	Viper's Bugloss	30	Monarch Dwarf	pink to purple
Eschscholtzia californica	Californian Poppy	21–45	Monarch Art Shades	lemon to orange
Godetia grandiflora	Godetia	21–60	Monarchs, Kelvedon Glory, etc	crimson, pinks, etc
Gypsophila elegans	Baby's Breath	45	*rosea*, Covent Garden, Monarch	white
Iberis umbellata	Candytuft	21–40	Fairy mixed, Red Flash	white, pinks, reds
Delphinium ajacis	Larkspurs	60–90	Giant Imperial, Hyacinth-flowered	blues, red rose, white
Lathyrus odoratus	Sweet Pea	to 240	selected strains, etc	very varied
Lavatera trimestris	Mallow	to 80	Tanagra, Loveliness	carmine rose
Lavia elegans	Tidy Tips	45–60	Cutting Gold	golden yellow
Linaria maroccana	Toad-flax	20	Fairy Bouquet	white, pink, red, etc
Linum grandiflorum	Flax	to 30	*rubrum*	crimson-scarlet
Matthiola bicornis	Night-scented Stock	30	species	lilac, scented
Nemophila insignis	Baby blue eyes	7.5	species	blue
Nicandra physaloides	Shoo Fly Plant	60–90	species	pale blue
Nigella damascena	Love-in-a-Mist	45	Persian Jewels, Miss Jekyll	blues, pinks
Phacelia campanularia		25	Blue Bonnets	blue
Papaver rhoeas	Shirley Poppy	60–75	Paeony-flowered, Rev. Wilks	scarlet, pink, etc
Reseda odorata	Mignonette	30–45	Goliath, Machet	reddish shades
Scabiosa atropurpurea	Pincushion flower	45–90	Dwarf Double, Monarch Cockade	blue, pink, purple
Helianthus annuus	Sunflower	2–3m	Autumn Beauty, Sungold	yellow to gold
Tropaeolum majus	Nasturtium	22–30	Gleam, Jewel, Red Roulette	yellow, orange, red
Half-Hardy Annuals				
*Ageratum houstonianum**	Floss Flower	12–20	F_1 hybs, Blue Mink, etc	blue, white
Amaranthus tricolor	Joseph's Coat	38–75	Early Splendour, Illumination	Reddened foliage
*Antirrhinum majus**	Snapdragon	30–60	Tom Thumb, nanum, Tetra, etc	very varied
Arctosis grandis	African Daisy	to 60	large-flowered hybrids	white, yellow, orange
Callistephus chinensis	China Aster	21–60	dwarf, Pompone, Duchess, etc	white, blues, pinks, etc
Celosia argentea	Cockscomb	30–60	*cristata*, *plumosa* vs	gold, pink, scarlet
Coreopsis tinctoria	Tickweed	to 50	Baby Sun	golden-yellow
Cosmos bipannatus	Cosmea	60–90	Klondyke vs, Sensation	yellows, to red
Felicia bergeriana	Kingfisher Daisy	15	species	blue
Gomphrena globosa	Globe Amaranth	30	nanacompacta 'Buddy'	white, red, purple

Botanical name	Common name	Height in cm	Notable varieties	Colours
Helichrysum bracteatum	Straw-flower	30	Monarch Spangle, Hot Bikini	varied, red
*Impatiens sultani**	Busy Lizzie	45	F$_1$ hybs, Ziz Zag	red, orange, pinks
Ipomoea tricolor	Morning Glory	300	Heavenly Blue, Scarlet O'Hara	blue, red
Kochia scoparia	Summer Cypress	60	*trichophylla* (Burning Bush)	foliage russeted
Lobelia erinus	Lobelia	10–15	Cambridge Blue, etc	blue, white
Matricaria eximia	Feverfew	20–25	White Stars, Golden Ball	white, yellow,
Mesembryanthemum criniflorum	Livingstone daisy	7cm	mixed	pink, buff, mauve, etc
Nemesia strumosa	Nemesis	25–30	Monarch, Unwin, strains	varied, brilliant
*Nicotiana affinis**	Tobacco Plant	30–75	F$_1$ Crimson Rock, Top Arts, etc	crimson, white, etc
*Petunia hybrida**	Petunia	15–40	F$_1$ hybs, grandiflora, etc	varied and many
Phlox drummondii	Phlox	15–30	grandiflora, nana compacta	bright, varied
Portulaca grandiflora	Sun Plant, Rose Moss	15	Daydream, F$_1$ Sunglo	white, red, yellow
Rudbeckia hirta vs	Cone Flower	60	Rustic Dwarfs, Marmalade	orange, browns
Salpiglossis sinuata	Tube Tongue	45–60	F$_1$ Splash, F$_2$ Bolero	crimson, yellow, pinks
Salvia splendens	Scarlet Sage	23–30	Rodeo, Blaze of Fire, Panorama	scarlet, violet
Statice sinuata	Sea Lavender	38–45	Art Shades	rose, orange, carmine
Tagetes erecta	African Marigold	60–90	F$_1$ hybs, Climax, Jubilee, etc	yellows
Tagetes patula	French Marigold	15–30	Mariettavs, Petite vs, etc	yellows, orange
Tagetes tenuifolium	Mexican Marigold	15	Monarch vs, Golden Gem	lemon, golden
Verbena × hybrida	Vervain	10–40	Sparkle, Royal Bouquet	red, blue, pink
Zinnia elegans	Youth and Old Age	15–30	Thumbelina, Peter Pan, Ruffles	varied

A Pick of Biennials

Botanical name	Common name	Height in cm	Notable varieties	Colours
Campanula medium	Canterbury Bell	45–90	calycanthema, Dwarf vs	blue, white
Cheiranthus allionii	Siberian Wallflower	38	Apricot Delight, Golden Bedder	yellows
*Cheiranthus cheiri**	Wallflower	23–30	Harper Crewe, Monarch	very varied
Digitalis purpurea	Foxglove	120–150	Excelsior hybs	pink, white, etc
*Dianthus barbatus**	Sweet William	25–60	Monarch, Messenger	pink, white, etc
*Dianthus caryophyllus**	Carnation	30–60	Chaubaud Giant, Enfant de Nice	reds, pinks, etc
Lunaria annua (*biennis*)	Honesty, Moonwort	50–60	v variegata, alba	purple, white
Matthiola sinuata	Stock	45	E. Lothian, Brompton	rose, white, etc
Myosotis alpestris	Forget-me-Not	15–25	Blue Ball, Carmine King, etc	blue, carmine
Oenothera biennis	Evening Primrose	to 75	native species	yellow
Oenothera trichocalyx	Evening Primrose	45		white, scented
Papaver nudicaule	Iceland Poppy	45–60	F$_1$ Champagne Bubbles	varied
Saliva sclarea	Clary	90–120	v turkestanica	bluish white

* technically perennials, best grown as biennials

9
Value from Vegetables

Money-saving is an important incentive in growing your own vegetables. But the real value from vegetables lies in the superior food quality of fresh produce in vitamins, food-minerals, and potential flavour. You can also grow those kinds not readily available or which are expensive at the shops.

Intensive vegetable cropping requires careful planning and attention to detail. It is unlikely you will be able to grow every vegetable successfully. Your soil, situation, and environment will impose limitations. Start simply, with the hardiest and strong-growing crops, suited to your soil and locality. Good carrots do not grow on clay. Globe artichokes and outdoor tomatoes and exotics like sweet corn need sun and warmth to do well. Check your area to ascertain if it is prone to 'fly' infestation before you go overboard on onions, carrots or turnips. Do see that your soil is free of the finger-and-toe or clubroot fungus before you crop with brassicas, the cabbage tribe.

Plan a Rotation   A rotation of crops means growing each one on a different piece of ground each year. The only exception is onions. This conserves soil fertility. It lessens the risk of pests or diseases building up. It enables the most economical and efficient use of labour, organic manures, lime and fertilizers. The simplest rotation is a 3–year cycle.

Roughly, divide the area into 3 equal plots. Plot 1 is cropped with early potatoes (followed by spring cabbage, leeks, turnips after lifting), and maincrop potatoes. Plot 2 is cropped with cabbage, cauliflower, brussels sprouts, kale; intercropped with saladings; beans, and peas. Plot 3 is cropped with root vegetables, beetroot, carrots, parsnips, salsify, parsley, and annual herbs. Onions can have a separate piece where they can be grown in successive years, or be included on plot 3.

In the second year, plot 1 is cropped as plot 2; plot 2 as plot 3; and plot 3 as plot 1. In the third year, plot 1 as plot 3, plot 2 as plot 1, and plot 3 as plot 2. In the fourth year, the cycle begins again as for the first year.

Raising the Crops Several vegetables are raised from seeds sown where they are to grow; chiefly broad beans, French beans, runner beans, peas, beetroot, carrots, lettuce, onions, parsnips, radish, spinach, swedes, and turnips. They are best sown when the soil is drying out and workable, and the soil temperature rising from 16–18°C/60–65°F. Sow by soil conditions rather than by the calendar. Too wet or too cold a soil means failures. Seeds sown closely together will need thinning at the seedling stage. A march of one to three weeks may be stolen on the season by sowing under cover of glass or plastic cloches which raise soil temperature by 2–3°C/4–6°F, and give protection.

Other crops such as brassicas, celery, leeks and lettuce may be raised from seeds in seed boxes, or in seed-beds and the seedlings subsequently transplanted to where they are to grow when developing their first true leaves. Plants of frost-susceptible crops such as cucumber, marrow, melon, sweet corn, and tomato may be raised singly from seeds in small peat-fibre pots or soil-blocks in a heated frame or greenhouse in March–April and planted out without root disturbance in May or early June. Or they can be bought in from nurserymen.

A Choice of Vegetables The kind of vegetables to grow will be chosen to suit personal or family preferences. Make a note of these first, then you can refer to the seed catalogues of repute and select the varieties, with particular attention to their suitability for your garden. Discount hyperbole a little in descriptions, and in doubt give preference to selected strains of growers' time-tested varieties. New strains and F_1 hybrids are being constantly introduced and should be tried for their suitability and performance in your own garden. Some salient points to help your choice and worth noting are:

Asparagus Perennial and permanent. Culture is specialised and should be studied. Best started with one year old plants in April; will crop 25 years or more. Varieties: Kidner's, Connover's Colossal; Sutton's Perfection, Paske's Regal strain.

Beans, Broad Hardy. Best sown February–April. Winter sowings chancy. Soil—pH6.5 +, with phosphates. Varieties: Longpod for hardiness; Windsor for bulk.

Beans, French Need warm sun, well-drained soil, available phosphates, and pH6.5 +. Varieties: Black Prince, Loch Ness, Tenderlong, King Horn Wax.

Beans, runner Need deep, well-drained, moisture-retentive soil; pH6.5–7. Frost-tender. Syringe often in hot weather. Varieties: Kelvedon Marvel, Achievement, Streamline, Sutton's Sunset.

Beetroot Need good loam, pH6.5. Varieties: Selected Globe, Boltardy, Cylindra, Detroit, Silver Seakale (for leaves).

Broccoli (Winter Cauliflower) Need humus-rich, firm soil, pH6.5. Varieties: for warm, coastal or southern gardens— Seale-Hayne strains, Angers No. 1–5, Snow-White; for colder areas—Veitch's Self-Protecting, Walcharen varieties; for autumn-maturing—Australian varieties.

Broccoli, sprouting Excellent, long-cropping, essential for spring. Reasonably good soil, pH6.5. Varieties: Calabrese; Purple Sprouting; White Sprouting.

Brussels sprouts Soil as for broccoli. Peer Gynt (early), Roodnerf vars, Fasolt are excellent varieties.

Cabbage Soil as for broccoli. Choose varieties for seasonal use: for summer–autumn: Golden Acre, Ballerina, Witham Pride, Rearguard; for winter—Winter Monarch, Christmas Drumhead, Savoy types (January King, Prince and Queen); for spring—April, Offenham vars, Wheeler's Imperial.

Carrot Needs porous, sandy loam type of soil, pH6–6.5. Varieties: Early Nantes, Nantes, Chantenay red-cored vars; Winter Monarch (heavy yield); St. Valery (maincrop).

Cauliflower Needs rich loam soil, firm, pH6.5–7. Varieties: All-The-Year-Round (successional sowings); Alpha vars; Mechelese vars; Snowball Early Super.

Celery Needs humus-rich, moist soil, pH6–6.5, deeply dug. Varieties: Giant Pink, Giant White, Golden Self-Blanching.

Celeriac Porous soil in good heart, pH6.5. Variety: Globus.
Cucumber (outdoor) Chiefly for warm localities, sunny summers. Best grown on low mounds of well-rotted organic material and soil, well watered and fed. Varieties: Bedfordshire Prize, Baton Vert, Perfection, Venlo Pickling (Gherkins).
Endive Needs light rich soil, pH6–6.5. Relative of Chicory. Sow late May; blanch for autumn–winter use. Variety: Batavian.
Globe Artichoke Needs well-drained loam, pH6–6.5; warm localities. Allow $1.2m^2$/48in per plant, for 12 'buds' per plant; crop 3 years and then renew.
Jerusalem Artichoke Succeeds on poor soils. Makes good temporary fence. Grow from root tubers, planted 15cm/6in deep, March. Gives edible tubers for winter. 2m/80in tall.
Kale (Borecole) Hardy green for winter, grown as for cabbage. Varieties: Cottager's, Scotch Curled.
Kohlrabi Bulbous-stemmed cabbage, grown as cabbage. Variety: Earliest White.
Leek Adaptable to most soils, but prefers deep loam, pH6–6.5. Raise seedlings to drop singly in holes 15cm/6in deep, 15cm/6in apart, in June, filling with water; or in 15cm/6in deep trenches. Varieties: Catalina, Musselburgh, Giant Winter, The Lyon, Titan.
Lettuce, cabbage Moisture-retentive, humus-rich soil, pH6.5. March–April sowing varieties: Fortune, Suzan, Windermere; May: Avondefiance, Webbs Wonderful; Great Lakes, Salad Bowl; August–September: Cobham Green, Valdor, Imperial Winter, Arctic King.
Lettuce, cos Similar soil as for cabbage lettuce. Varieties: March–April sowing: Little Gem, Lobjoits Green, Winter Density, Paris White; September–October sowing: Lobjoits Green, Winter Density, Vaux's Self Folding.
Marrow (including gourds, courgettes, pumpkins) Need stations or mounds of half rotted organic matter, half soil, no lime. Plant up in June. Varieties: trailing—Little Gem, Long Green, Long White; Vegetable Spaghetti; bush—Green Bush, White Bush, Golden Zucchini, Green bush Courgette, Custard Yellow, Hundredweight Pumpkin.
Onions Humus-rich, well-drained and sunned soil, pH6–6.5. Most easily grown from 'sets', planted February–March,

varieties: Coranado, Stuttgarter Giant. Or from seeds sown in March; varieties: Ailsa Craig, Bedfordshire Champion, Hygro, Autumn Queen. For spring onions—White Lisbon; for pickling—Barletta, The Queens. For August sowing and over-wintering: Japanese vars Express Yellow, Imai Yellow.

Parsnip Need deep, porous, lightish soil, pH6.5–7. Sow February–April. Varieties: White Gem, Tender and True, Avonresister, Offenham.

Peas Need deeply dug soil, high in phosphates and lime, pH6.5. Varieties: for March–April sowing—Meteor, Kelvedon Viscount, Feltham First, Pilot Improved. Second early varieties, sown late March onwards—Hurst Beagle, Hurst Green Shaft, Onward Improved, Kelvedon Monarch, Achievement; tall maincrops: Miracle, Alderman, Lord Chancellor, Petit Pois (Gullivert), Purple Podded and Asparagus Pea are novelties.

Potatoes Return most food value per m^2/yd^2. Best soils are porous, humus-rich, but crop well on most soils except chalk, given plenty of organic manure or compost, and a pH5.5–6.5. Select virus-free seed tubers, and 'sprout' by exposing eye-end up to light in frost-proof shed or greenhouse. Varieties: early—Duke of York, Foremost, Arran Pilot, Epicure. Second Early—Dunbar Rover, Pentland Javelin, Craigs Royal, Redskin; Maincrop—Maris Peer, Dr Mackintosh, Majestic, Arran Banner, Dunbar Standard.

Radish Need humus-rich, porous soil, pH6.5–7. Sow March onwards, useful as catch-crop and to mix with slower germinating seeds such as onions, parsley, etc, to mark position of rows. Varieties: Cherry Belle, Scarlet Globe, French Breakfast, Long White Icicle; and for July sowing for winter use: China Rose, Black Spanish.

Salsify Easily grown in porous soils, pH6.5. Variety: Sutton's Giant. Sow April, for winter use of roots, known as the Vegetable Oyster.

Shallot Needs humus-rich, firm soil, pH6–6.5. Grown from 'sets' placed half their depth in the soil in February or March, harvested July. Varieties: Champagne Early, Dutch Yellow, Giant Yellow.

Spinach Needs well-drained, humus-rich soil, pH6.5. Sow summer spinach February to August, in vars Hurst's 101,

Supergreen, Viroflay; winter spinach in August–September, in vars Long Standing Prickly, Greenmarket. Spinach Leaf Beet can be sown in April, or mid-August.

Sweetcorn (Maize)   Needs porous, humus-rich soil, pH6–6.5, warm sun. Harvest when silky tassels wither. Varieties: Earliking, Kelvedon Glory, John Innes Hybrid, Golden Bantam.

Tomato, outdoor   A gamble north of the Midlands except in mild, sunny localities. Needs humus-rich soil, well-drained, pH6, adequate in potassium. Plant out late May–early June. Associates well with sweetcorn, but not with potatoes. Varieties: Ailsa Craig, Alicante, Moneymaker, Outdoor Girl, Golden Queen; and Bush varieties Sigmabush, French Cross, Amateur, and Sleaford Abundance.

Turnip (and Swede)   Need rich porous loam, pH6.5–7. Sow April–July. Varieties: Golden Ball, Milan White, Manchester Market, Red Top Milan, Tokyo Cross.

The Herb Patch   Choose a patch of well-drained ground, enrich with leaf-mould or well-rotted peat or ground bark; does not need to be rich. Buy in plants of perennials such as **pot marjoram, sage, sweet savory, tarragon,** and culinary **thyme** in March–April; or grow from shoot cuttings taken in April–May. Buy **mint** roots in late winter, plant where their growth can be confined, such as a bottomless old bucket, or plastic ring culture pot, sunk in the soil. Make sowings of annuals such as **basil, borage, coriander, dill, sweet marjoram, parsley, summer savory**, and biennial **caraway** in March–April. Plant bulbs of **chives** early in the year in small groups to form clumps.

10
Tree Fruits, Soft Fruits and Strawberries

Welcome health-giving crops of fruits can be grown in gardens year after year given patience, and a willingness to master management techniques. You will probably have to wait 2 to 4 years before you pick fruits from apple, pear or stone fruit trees; two years before you can harvest currants, gooseberries, raspberries and bramble berries from soft fruit bushes or plants, and a year before you can gather your first worthwhile harvest of strawberries.

The site for fruit is important, and should be open, sun-warmed, sheltered from strong winds, and on reasonably high ground from which cold air at freezing temperatures can flow readily. The soil needs to be reasonably well-drained, porous in depth, with sufficient clay and humus colloids to foster moisture and nutrient retention, and on the acid side (pH6–6.5). It would be wise to defer planting on waterlogged, dry and chalky or limy soils until they can be improved (see Chapter 2).

TREE FRUITS

Where there is room it makes care and management easier if you plant fruit trees together, with like kinds and varieties near to each other. Fruit trees are propagated vegetatively, by grafting the scion or shoot of the chosen variety which subsequently develops into the stem and top growth, on a rootstock near the base. The rootstock is chosen to develop early fruiting and to modify growth, with increased disease resistance.

As they are deciduous, planting time for all fruit trees lasts from late October to March, given agreeable weather and soil conditions. Each tree needs to be set in well-dug soil, with roots evenly spread, staked if necessary, covered and firmed with topsoil laced with bonemeal and sifted compost or similar organic material, and with the graft union above ground. A top dressing of organic material helps, but no rich fertilizing while roots are getting established in the first year.

Apples are grown as standards and half- or short standards on vigorous rootstocks (MXXV, MM104, or MM111), which can best be planted as specimen trees. For gardens, apples on dwarfing rootstocks (MIX, MVII or MM106) come into bearing sooner and fit limited space. The most suitable forms are bush trees, planted 3–3.5m/10–12ft apart; single-stemmed cordons at 190cm/76in apart, in rows 2m/6½ft apart; and trained espaliers at 3.5–4m/12–14ft apart, to be grown by paths or on walls. One other form is offered as the 'family' tree, consisting of about three compatible varieties grafted on to the same plant; to be grown as a specimen tree.

Ensuring Fruit   Some apples are not very fertile, and all bear better when cross-pollinated, which is ensured by planting varieties that flower at the same period, choosing at least one pollinating variety to six of a preferred kind. Secondly, ensure that chosen varieties are likely to do well in your area, being hardy and escaping spring frosts. Avoid Cox's in cold and northern gardens. A good short list is shown on opposite page.

Management calls for intelligent pruning, feeding, and disease/pest prevention and control.

Pruning to encourage strong new shoot growth to shape the tree is done in winter; cutting severely to induce strong new growth, moderately just to extend main stems steadily. Pruning to induce flower (fruit) bud formation is done in summer, mid-July to early September; when lateral shoots are reduced to a third or fourth leaf from their base. Prune weak shoots more severely than strong; remove sick or dead growth when seen; remove unwanted criss-crossing shoots entirely to base.

Early Flowering	Use in	Mid-season Flowering	Use in	Late Flowering	Use in
Laxton's Fortune: D	Sept	Merton Knave: D	Aug–Sep	Orlean's Reinette: D	Nov–Feb
Egremont Russet: D	Oct–Dec	Cox's Orange: D	Oct–Dec	Worcester Pearmain: D	Sep–Oct
Lord Lambourne: D	Oct–Nov	Ellison's Orange: D	Sep–Oct	Crawley Beauty: C	Oct–Apl
Sunset: D	Oct–Dec	Laxton's Superb: D	Jan–Mar	Edward VII: C	Oct–Apl
Rev. W. Wilks: C	Sep–Dec	James Grieve: D	Sep		
Arthur Turner: C	Jul–Sep	Charles Ross: C/D	Sep–Nov		
		Lane's Prince Albert: C	Oct–Feb		
		Bramley's Seedling: C	Oct–Mar		
		Grenadier: C	Aug–Sep		

C = Culinary var; D = Dessert var

Feeding calls for an annual top-dressing of organic material in winter, and a base fruit fertilizer in February–March, bearing in mind that culinary varieties need rather more nitrogen than dessert, which need adequate potassium.

Disease and pest prevention spraying can be sensibly based on (a) tar oil emulsion in winter to destroy aphid eggs and clean trees of lichen and moss; (b) pre-blossom fungicidal spray to control scab, (c) repeated after petal-fall, plus an insecticide against emerging pests. This is supplemented by taking prompt action at the first signs of trouble during the growing season. Manufacturers' handbooks should be studied for their recommendations and products.

Pears Culture is much the same as for apples, but they are less tolerant of dry, cold, wet and chalky soils, and need warm sun to ripen well, especially dessert kinds; and are likely to do best on well sunned walls in the north or in sheltered warm corners. Pears are usually grafted on the Malling Quince A or B rootstocks, and available in bush, cordon and horizontal-trained espaliers for gardens.

If only one variety is planted, it must be self-fertile Conference. But like apples, pears do best where cross-pollinating can take place between varieties flowering at the same period. A good short list is shown on following page.

Management is much on the lines as for apples, but with slight differences. In pruning for flower bud formation, cutting should begin 7 to 14 days earlier, and can be somewhat more severe, beginning in late June. Feeding calls for a fertilizer rather high in nitrogen, as for culinary apples. Preventive

85

Early Flowering	Use in	Mid-season Flowering	Use in	Late Flowering	Use in
Louise Bonne de Jersey: D	Oct	Conference: D/C	Oct–Nov	Beurre Hardy: D	Oct
Durondeau: D	Oct–Nov	Emile d'Heyst: D	Oct–Nov	Bristol Cross: D	Sep–Oct
Improved Fertility: C/D	Sep–Oct	Josephine de Malines: D	Dec–Jan	Doyenne du Comice: D	Nov–Dec

C = Cullinary var; D = Dessert var

spraying is similar, but the spring applications need to be made earlier, in timing with flowering.

Harvesting Apples are gathered ripe, when the stalk parts from the twig on being lifted horizontal. Pears are gathered unripe and green, when a lift and a twist breaks them loose. Early pears ripen in a few days indoors, at 15.5–18°C/60–65°F. Keeping apples and pears needs cool, well-ventilated and somewhat moist storing conditions. Choice fruits can be wrapped individually in oiled papers.

STONE FRUITS

These are less amenable to dwarfing rootstocks, and tend to make somewhat large, sprawly trees. All like well-drained, loamy soils, with chalk or lime and a warm garden with a fair amount of summer sun. The easiest to grow are the plums and damsons on Brompton or St. Julian A rootstock, as bushes, spaced 4–5m/14–16ft apart, choosing the self-fertile varieties—Victoria plum, Merryweather damson, and Denniston's Superb Gage, to which you can then add the less certain croppers such as Early Laxton, Czar, Rivers Early Prolific and Pershore Yellow Egg plums, and the Farleigh damson, as fancied. But other varieties, especially the gages such as Early Transparent, Jefferson's, Oullin's Golden, and Kirke's Blue plum—all delectable fruit—are most likely to bear well in sheltered sunny localities. Under favourable conditions, the peaches Peregrine, Duke of York, and Rochester can be grown as bushes like the plums, only requiring more room, spaced 6m/20ft apart.

When bush-grown, prune these stone fruits when in active growth: (1) in spring, when leading extension shoots of framework branches are cut back to above a suitable bud;

Modern hybrid tea roses come in almost every colour and many are famous for their scent

lightly if growth is strong, more severely if weak; (2) cut out moribund, weak or criss-crossing lateral shoots, and shorten over-vigorous ones by pinching out the tips.

Feeding should consist of organic manuring of the roots in winter, with basic slag or bonemeal every fourth year, and a balanced fruit fertilizer each February or March.

Pests, rather than a disease, menace stone fruits growing well. They should receive a winter tar oil wash, and an insecticidal spray or dust to prevent caterpillar ravages after petal-fall. Other pests or diseases should be dealt with quickly as they arise.

The only truly hardy fruitful cherry for most gardens is the self-fertile Morello, yielding sour fruits for culinary use, on rootstock Malling F/12/1 to be grown as a bush, spaced at 5m/16½ft, or a fan-shaped tree on a high wall, even one facing the north. Sweet cherries, however, are only for areas south and east of the Severn-Humber line on the map, and sunny, warm gardens with well-drained porous loamy soil, with lime or chalk. Bushes need 7m/23ft between them.

SOFT FRUITS

These comprise the currants and the spiny stemmed, related gooseberries, which are grown as low bushes; the raspberries, blackberries and related hybrid berries which fruit on canes produced anew each year and need to be grown on supports; and strawberries which are stoloniferous perennial herbs. They come into bearing more quickly than tree fruits, crop prolifically and more certainly, and require less space. High in vitamins and minerals, though low in calories, the soft fruits help greatly to vary and enrich the family diet.

Blackcurrants are very hardy and succeed on most soils enriched with humus material and kept well supplied with nitrogen. Propagated by cuttings of young shoots, bushes of 1, 2 or 3 years may be planted in October to March, in mild conditions, about 1.5m/5ft apart, and all shoots are then cut to within 8–12cm/3–4½in of soil level. Fruit is borne on shoots grown the previous year. No crop can be expected in the first year after planting, but thereafter bushes should yield annually.

No garden would be complete without a patch
of crocuses in the spring

Management   After the first year's growth, cut back every other new shoot to just above a bud near the base after leaf-fall to foster more shoots. Thereafter, cut the shoots as soon as they have fruited to just above strong new forming lateral shoots, and cut one or more of the oldest branches back almost to ground level. This keeps new shoots, which bear the finest fruits, coming forward.

Feed generously to nurture the new growth—organic material to the roots in winter, a compound fertilizer high in nitrogen each February.

Winter spray with tar oil wash to control aphids. Keep a watch for abnormally swollen buds, indicative of big-bud-mite infestation, and when seen spray with lime-sulphur or endosulphan when flower-buds are like tiny bunches of green grapes and about to open.

Red and Whitecurrants are differently coloured fruiting varieties of the same species. Need well-drained porous soil, humus-rich, well provided with potassium, and of pH6–6.5; a warm, sunned position, sheltered from high winds. Differ from blackcurrants as although grown from cuttings, they are grown as bushes in short single main stems, less often as cordons; and also fruit chiefly on short spurs from the old wood growth at the base of young shoots formed the previous year. Planting time is between October and March in mild conditions, bushes being spaced 1.2m/4ft apart.

Management   To prune cut back all side shoots to five leaves at the end of June, and again to within $1.25cm/\frac{1}{2}$in of their base in winter. Shorten leading shoots of main branches by one-third to one-half in winter.

Winter spray with tar oil wash in December or January, against aphids. Top-dress with organic material each winter, and give a fruit fertilizer adequate in potash, as for dessert apples, in February or March. Although self-fertile, the plants flower in April and on nights when frost is forecast, cover with polythene or sacking.

Gooseberries differ from their relatives, the currants, in that they can produce fruits on young shoots of the previous year's growth *and* on spurs on the older stems. They can be grown as bushes, as short-stemmed bush trees, or as cordons. Plant as for currants, 1.5m/5ft apart with 2–3-year-old bushes. Need good drainage, and like a humus-rich, loamy soil, pH6–6.5, with open positions.

Management Young plants should have all shoots pruned severely in the first year to induce a strong framework of branches. Thereafter, summer pruning, after fruiting, can consist of cutting back lateral shoots lightly if strong, more severely if weak; and in winter thinning out criss-crossing, inward-growing shoots, and shortening the leaders. Cordons are pruned after fruiting by reducing all laterals to 4 or 5 leaves, and then to within 2–3cm/1–1½in of the base in winter; and tipping the extension leader.

In feeding, emphasis should be on potassium—a good top-dressing of organic material in winter, and a fruit fertilizer rich in potash, as for dessert apples and red and white-currants in February. Gooseberries should be included in the application of tar oil wash to control aphids. American mildew can be troublesome in spring and need fungicidal control with benomyl.

Raspberries need a soil with good drainage, very liberally enriched with humus-forming organic matter, of pH6, in sun or light shade, and are planted 45–60cm/18–24in apart, in rows 2m/6½ft apart, where the shoots may be tied to wire supports, strained on posts about 1.5–2m/5–6½ft high. Planting time is November–December, though often planted later to February. Young single canes are set about 7cm/2½in deep, and cut back to within 2–3 buds of soil level. New canes then grow the first year, to fruit the next, and are tied to the wires.

Management A cane, or plant or stool, throws at least 2 canes the first year, four the next. After fruiting, the fruited canes are cut at soil level, and the strongest new canes, up to six per stool, trained in for the following year. Autumn-fruiting varieties, however, have their fruited canes cut away in February–March.

Feeding calls for rotted organic material, peat or ground bark each winter; an organic-based compound fertilizer in February–March, and organic litter mulches in the growing season. Lime is not usually necessary, and a well-cared for planting will fruit for 15 years or more. No routine preventive pesticide applications are needed, but the raspberry beetle, responsible for grub-infested fruits, may need to be controlled by a derris insecticide applied in June.

Blackberries and Hybrids Cultivated blackberries and their related hybrid bramble fruits yield superior and heavier crops than those in the wild. They succeed on most soils which are reasonably well-drained and enriched with humus-forming organic materials. Planting time is October to March, when soil conditions and weather are favourable.

They may be grown on a row of wires, strained to posts 2m/6½ft tall, and set 2m/6½ft apart. They are decorative enough to be planted on walls, fences, over pergolas, trellis, arches or to clamber up old trees.

Management Plant with crown bud(s) just covered with soil and cut back existing cane to 15cm/6in. Train and fasten the new canes for future fruiting. Prune by cutting out fruited shoots each autumn. With loganberries and hybrid brambles, the fruited canes are removed to base each year, as with raspberries. An organic top-dressing to the roots in autumn–early winter, and an organic-based fertilizer, high in nitrogen, in February or March, sustains strong growth and high yields.

Strawberries should be planted in beds to grow and crop for four years; then make a fresh start on fresh ground. Like soils with good drainage, very liberally enriched with humus-forming organic matter, and steady-acting organic fertilizers (hoof and horn, bonemeal, powdered seaweed in equal parts), pH6; with an open position in sun or light shade, and as free from late spring frosts as possible.

Best planting time in August–October, with 1-year pot-grown plants, to start fruiting the following year. May also be planted in March–April, but should not be allowed to fruit in the same year. Set plants carefully and firmly with crowns at surface level, spacing 30–45cm/12–18in apart, in rows 60cm/24in apart.

Management Water in a dry spring. In late May lay flat straw mats or black sheet polythene, weighted down with stones, beneath plants, after rain, to obtain clean fruits, and net against birds. After harvest, remove all covers; cut off runner stems except one or two of the strongest to train in line between plants to root and make new plants; cut off old leaves for burning; and suppress weeds by hoeing or using a contact herbicide. In late autumn, give an organic based fertilizer and liberal top-dressing of organic humus material. No routine preventive sprays or dusts are needed, but prompt action should be taken in growing period when trouble arises— against aphids and red spider mites with derris insecticides; against botrytis grey mould or mildew with benomyl or thiram fungicides; against slugs, snails and strawberry seed beetles with methiocarb pellets.

11
Keeping the Garden Healthy

It is natural for plants to grow lustily and healthily in fulfilling their seasonal growth and life cycles. Given a favourable environment and good culture they do so, even under the somewhat contrived and artificial conditions of a civilised man's garden.

Nevertheless, plants are only one group, though large and highly important, of organisms among the myriad of organisms that populate and make a battlefield of our planet in unceasing cycles of life and death. As living organisms, plants are subject to attack by parasites which seek them as sources of food and energy, destroying them if unchecked, and which we regard as disastrous infections and pests.

Keeping the garden healthy falls into two parts: (1) providing the plants we grow with conditions most conducive to fostering their vigour; and (2) taking the right action to control unwanted parasites at the earliest possible moment.

Environmental Factors Many garden plants are more vulnerable to parasites since we grow them far from the natural balance of their native habitat. Others are selected, hybridised cultivated varieties unknown in the wild and need good culture to thrive. Our practice of growing similar plants *en bloc* or closely together invites the fast propagation and multiplication of their parasites.

Resistance to parasitic attacks is implicit in good culture— the placing and spacing of plants so that they receive the light and air that dispels dank darkness and stagnancy favourable to many parasitic fungi and pests.

The Nature of Plant Diseases   Most of these are caused by fungi, germinating from air-borne, water-borne, or carrier-borne spores, invading the plant host tissues to feed, grow and produce spore-forming bodies for their further advance. Others are caused by bacteria which gain access usually through a lesion, cut or wound. Some by viruses.

Against fungal diseases, fungicides are used—chemicals chosen for their toxicity to the fungi without impairing the plant, or, hopefully, imperilling the gardener, children or pets. By and large they are more effective in halting spore germination than killing the fungus itself. They, therefore, need to be applied to cover not only the fungus but also all surfaces of the plant exposed to spore contamination. It follows that fungicides are most effective when applied evenly either just before infection is heralded (as with potato blight) or in the early stages of attack. As fungi can recover very quickly, a second or a third application at 7–10 day intervals is often needed.

Weather conditions influence infections; botrytis grey mould, and leaf moulds flourish in the damp and humid, mildews and rusts in heat and dryness. It is sensible to seek expert identification and advice when trouble is baffling, and highly important to read the maker's instructions and notes before applying the product.

Fungicides are prepared as concentrated solutions for dilution, or as emulsions or wettable powders, from which dilute solutions or suspensions can be made for application by spray, or syringe. It is worthwhile investing in a pressure sprayer of a size compatible with the work likely to be done. Fitted with a fine nozzle, this puts out a mist-like spray of good covering power, and if thoroughly washed and cleaned after each use, should last years.

Fungicides are also put up in powder form for application as small dust-clouds to settle on plant surfaces, supplied either in puffer packs for ready application or in bulk for use with dusting or blowing appliances.

Most fungicides work at the surface of plants, and cover needs to be given as new growth is made, or to make good depletion by weather. Some new fungicides enter the sap stream and plant tissues and are termed systemic, attacking the parasitic fungus as it invades. The chief fungicides for garden use, worth having on hand are as follows:

Fungicides for the Garden

Chemical name	Typical Brands	Forms available	Diseases controlled
Benomyl (systemic)	Benlate	wettable powder	Fungus diseases of fruits, flowers, vegetables, moulds, mildews, etc
Bordeaux Mixture (copper-lime mix)	Murphy	powder	Grey mould, blight, and many common plant diseases
Captan	Orthocide 'P.P.' Captan 50	wettable powder	Fruit scab, Rose black spot, strawberry grey mould
		powder	Seed dressing against damping-off
Dichlofluanid	Elvaron (Bayer) Elvaron (M and B)	wettable powder	Botrytis grey mould on fruits rose black spot, cane spots, etc
Dinocap (Karathane)	Crotothane Midox Dinocap Murphy Dinocap 'P.P.' Karathane	liquid or wettable powder	powdery mildews on apple, soft fruits, cucumber, chrysanthemum, grape vines, and roses
Formaldehyde (Formalin)	Formasan Steriform	liquid	soil-borne fungus diseases, used as a soil sterilant
Lime Sulphur	Bentley's	liquid	Scab on tree fruits; gooseberry mildew
Mercurous chloride (Calomel)	Synchemicals MC Merfusan	liquid	Turf diseases, fusarium, corticium, dollar spot, etc
	Cyclosan Dust Murphy Calomel Dust PBI Calomel Dust	powder	Club root control in brassicas
Sulphur	Bayer Wettable 'P.P.' Spersul	wettable powder	Powdery mildews on tree and soft fruits, flowers, etc
	Bentley's Green Bentley's Yellow	Dust	Powdery mildews
Thiabendazole (systemic)	Tecto PPH	wettable powder	Powdery mildew, apple scab, turf diseases
Thiram (dithiocarbamate)	'P.P.' Ferna-col	Colloidal liquid	Botrytis grey mould, rusts, tulip fire, pear scab, etc
	'P.P.' Fernasan A	powder	seed-dressing against damping-off, foot-rot, etc
Zineb (dithiocarbamate)	PBI Dithane Murphy Zineb 'P.P.' Zineb 'UGS' Zineb A	wettable powder	Potato blight, botrytis grey mould, leaf mouid, downy mildews, leaf spots, rusts, etc

Virus Diseases   Viruses are extremely minute organisms that infect all parts of the plant, systemically via the sap. The outward symptoms are usually the crinkling of leaves, a mottling mosaic of yellow, grey, white leaf colour, stunted growth, weak, often discoloured flowers, inferior performance and cropping. As, as yet, there is no cure for a virus-sick plant, it should be completely uprooted and burnt to safeguard healthy plants. The virus can be transmitted by infected plant material, by the hands and implements after contact with diseased plants, or by sap-sucking insects such as aphids transferring from sick to healthy plants. A wide range of plants, flowers and fruits are virus-vulnerable. Our chief weapons are to plant only healthy, virus-free stock; practise good hygiene in the garden, and keep the insects vectors or carriers under control.

Plant Pests These are the animal organisms that feed on garden plants and are apt to increase in ratio to the food supply available. They include various insects and/or their larvae; slow-moving myriopods such as millipedes; spider mites; crustaceans such as woodlice; molluscs such as slugs and snails; and sometimes mice, voles and rabbits. While good hygienic practices, and sound culture go far in keeping plants thriving and vigorous, it is often necessary to take direct action to prevent pests decimating cherished plants or crops and bring them under control by the use of appropriate pesticides as insecticides, molluscides and parasiticides are often called.

Insecticides are applied to plants. They should destroy the pest without damaging the plant, not injure beneficial insects such as bees, and leave no persistent toxic residues to endanger pets or wild life, or to render food crops harmful to eat. Insecticides control pests either as contact poisons by direct application, or as stomach poisons applied to be ingested, either to the plant parts likely to be eaten, or to be absorbed by the plant into its sap and act systemically, particularly against sap-feeding aphids, thrips, spider mites and scale insects.

Insecticides may be used out of doors in the form of sprays, dusting powders, or aerosols. It is most efficient and economical to use them in anticipation of, or immediately, an attack develops. The aim is to disrupt the life cycle of the pest at a vulnerable stage, and is helpful to have some knowledge and recognition of the pests by study of an entomological text-book.

The safest to use as far as humans and animals are concerned are the organic-based derris and pyrethrum compounds, particularly on food crops, though there should be one or more days between the last application and harvest. No insecticide should be regarded as entirely safe. Hence the need to use them precisely and intelligently.

The above chart is a guide to some of the pesticides available to gardeners.

Pesticides for the Garden

Chemical name	Typical brands	Action	Form available	Harmful to
Carbaryl	Murphy Sevin Boots Sevin	stomachic	powder	Bees, fish
Derris (rotenone)	Bentley's Derris Murphy's Derris Abol Derris 1 Liquid Derris	stomachic stomachic stomachic stomachic	powder powder powder liquid	Fish
Dicofol acaricide	Murphy Kelthane 'P.P.' Kelthane	contact- stomachic	liquid	damaging to young plants
Malathion	Bentley's Dust Murphy's Dust PBI Malathexo Bentley's Liquid Murphy's Liquid PBI Liquid	contact- stomachic ,, ,, ,, ,,	powder ,, ,, liquid ,, ,,	bees, fish ,, ,, ,, ,, ,,
Metaldehyde molluscicide	Boots, May and Baker, Murphy, 'P.P.', Synchemicals Slug Pellets	contact- stomachic	pelleted with bait	animals, birds, children, game, fish
Menazon Systemic	'P.P.' Abol X	stomachic	colloidal liquid	Bees, animals, poultry
Methiocarb	Draza pellets PBI Draza G	contact- stomachic	pellets or granules	Fish, poultry
Nicotine	Bentley's Synchemical XL ALL	contact	liquid emulsion	humans, animals, fish, game, wild birds, bees, etc if contacted or inhaled
Pyrethrum	Py Powder Py Spray	contact	powder emulsion	bees ,,
Sulphur and lime-sulphur	Bentley's 'P.P.' Spersul	stomachic	liquid ,,	
Tar oil	Creebol, Mortegg	contact	liquid	fish

A FEW WORDS ABOUT WEEDS

Weeds, which have been well defined as plants growing where we do not want them, can take up a lot of time and effort in their suppression. They compete with garden plants for living space, air, sun, moisture and food to impair their growth and performance. They often harbour pests and diseases. They often offend aesthetically.

Chemical name	Chief Pests controlled	Minimum period between last application and harvest
Carbaryl	Codling, tortrix, winter moth caterpillars, capsid bugs, earwigs	7 days
Derris (rotenone)	Aphids, caterpillars, red spider mites, thrips, sawfly, raspberry beetle, etc	1 day
Dicofol acaricide	Red spider mites	2–7 days, according to crop
Malathion	Aphids, leaf hoppers, thrips, codling moth, red spider mites, sawfly, raspberry beetles, mealy bugs, scale insects, celery fly	4–7 days, as directed
Metaldehyde molluscicide	Slugs, snails	none, if applied correctly
Menazon Systemic	Aphids, sap-sucking insects	3 weeks
Methiocarb	Slugs, snails	7 days
Nicotine	Aphids, mealy bugs, thrips, white fly, capsid bugs, sawfly, woolly aphids, etc, by quick contact 'kill'	2 days
Pyrethrum	Quick knock-down of aphids, thrips, weevils, leaf beetles, etc	1 day but non-toxic ,,
Sulphur and lime-sulphur	Big-bud gall mites	follow maker's instructions
Tar oil	Over-wintering aphids and their eggs, and fruit pests	follow maker's instructions

Good control of weeds is possible by forking them out, cutting them down repeatedly, and by skilful use of the hoe and cultivator. The modern labour-saving way is to destroy them chemically, using weedkillers, or herbicides. They may be divided into four groups: total, residual, selective, and contact herbicides.

Total Weedkillers are toxic to all green plants (except algae, lichens and mosses), and are most useful in removing all vegetation from ground being brought into cultivation. They may be used selectively if strictly confined to the unwanted plants. Sodium chlorate (preferably with a fire-retardant additive) is most commonly used as Atlacide, or Nantcol; and is most effective when absorbed by the foliage and the roots. It disperses beyond the area of application, however, and should not be used within root-reach of garden plants. It is slow to clear, and treated ground is not safe for replanting for 3–9 months, according to dosage and drainage.

Ammonium sulphamate (Amcide) is used to kill trees, shrubs and clear scrub land, and also kills most herbaceous weeds and grasses. It is used in water solution to clear weed-infested ground, and scores over sodium chlorate in that it does not disperse from where it is applied and treated ground can be cultivated and planted within 12 weeks. Both sodium chlorate and ammonium sulphamate are safe and harmless to animal pets and birds, used correctly.

Residual Weedkillers These are based on water-insoluble chemicals, which lodge in the surface layer of the soil, decomposing only slowly, and thus control germinating weed seedlings and suppress much regrowth from perennial weed roots. They need to be applied to ground cleared of weed top growth, and give freedom from most common weeds for at least a season. They are most useful for paths and driveways, and areas being planted with established shrubs, trees, fruit bushes, roses, and perennials where the soil itself is not disturbed. Those for garden use are based on chloroxuron (Ciba/Geigy's 'Gesal' weed preventers for flower-beds, and vegetables); dichlobenil (Synchemicals 'Casoron G' granules); propachlor (Murphy Ramrod granules); or simazine (Murphy

Printop Rose Bed weedkiller), and for total weed suppression on paths, etc in Boots Path Weed Control; Gesal Weedex; Murphy Simazine; and 'P.P.' Pathclear).

Selective Weedkillers are based on chemicals which adversely affect broad-leaved dicotyledonous plants, but not the narrow-bladed monocotyledonous plants; and are largely used to control weeds in lawns. If used elsewhere, they must be confined to the weed plant. Many lawn weeds are controlled by herbicides based on 2,4–D (Ciba-Geigy 2,4–D Amine, Dicotox, Weedone LV 4, etc) or MCPA (Agroxone, Phenoxylene Plus, etc). Where clover is a problem mecoprop (Clovotox) may be used alone, or added to 2,4–D (Boots Lawn Weedkiller, Supertox, Verdone, Gesal Lawnweeder) or a 2,4–D plus dichlorprop (Selex, Murphy Lawn Weed Killer) is effective. Ioxynil (Actrilawn) is recommended for the quick control of seedling weeds in a newly germinated lawn; and where speedwells and parsley piert are troublesome in an established lawn ioxynil plus mecoprop (Iotox, Clovercide Extra) is a splendid wide spectrum weedkiller.

Couch, perennial and annual grasses, including bamboos, reeds and sedges, may be controlled by the application of a dalapon herbicide (Dowpon, 'P.P.' Dalapon, XL ALL Dalapon, etc) to their stems and foliage, allowing 4 to 6 weeks before cropping treated ground. Dalapon may be used to control unwanted grasses under hedges, under established fruit and ornamental trees, in asparagus beds, and where it can be confined to the plants to be controlled. Combined with MCPA (Hurstmaster) it makes a good total weedkiller on paths and ground not to be sown or planted for 8–10 weeks.

Tough-rooted weeds such as bindweed, and nettles, brambles, tree saplings, sucker growths, and brushwood is brought under control by herbicides containing 2,4,5–T (Boots Bramble and Nettle Killer, Phortox, Trioxone 50, SBK, Netlelex and Spontox), allowing at least 6 weeks to take full effect, and keeping grazing animals away from treated areas for at least 2 weeks.

Contact Herbicides are based on substances that destroy the chlorophyll, green-pigment in plants exposed to sunlight.

They act almost at once, causing the death of green plants
within a few days. They give good control of weeds growing
among garden plants where they can be applied by sprinkler
bar or shielded sprayer, to wet weeds without touching the
plants. The substances available are diquat (Reglone),
Paraquat (Gramoxone) and a combination of the two
(Weedol). Excess solution falling on the soil is promptly
neutralised and decomposed. This is the chemical equivalent
to hoeing.

Index

Air 8
Annuals 73, 75
Apples 84

Bark fibre 25
Biennials 74, 76
Blackberries 92
Blackcurrants 89
Boundaries 39
Bulbs 72

Cherries 89
Climate 10
Conifers 62
Corms 72
Cultivators 51

Digging 26
Diseases 95
Drainage 20

Fertilizers 27
Forks 50
Fruit 83
Fungicides 96

Garden features 34
Gooseberries 90

Hedges 55
   planting 58
   trimming 58
Herbicides 101

Herbs 82
Hoes 51
Hop manure 26
Humus 23

Lawns 45
Leaf mould 26
Light 8, 41

Minerals 13

Nutrient elements 9

Paths 44
Pears 85
Peat 25
Pesticides 98
Pests 97
Planting 39
Plums 86
Pruning 66

Rakes 51
Raspberries 91
Redcurrants 90
Roses 37
Rotation 77

Sewage sludge 26
Shears 52
Shrubs 63
Soil 11, 13–31
   acidity 21

  analysis 18
  calcareous 18
  clay 16
  gravel 15
  loam 16
  peat 18
  reclaimed 18
  sandy 16
  silty 16
  stony 15
Spades 50
Strawberries 92

Tools 49
Trees 60
Trowels 51

Vegetables 77
Virus diseases 96

Warmth 9
Water 8
Weedkillers 100
Weeds 99
Wheelbarrows 52
Whitecurrants 90
Wind 41